Peanut Butter Cookies

oven 350°

together: 1/2 C. butter or margarine (I use margarine)
1/2 C. peanut butter
1/2 C. white sugar
1/2 C. brown sugar

1 egg   tsp vanilla
1/2   tsp salt
1/2   tsp ...king so...

Mustard Sa...

white cidar vinegar

...e sugar.

mustard

...BS   yolks – well

untill thick.

...d butter

bo...

receipe

Auntie Maine's Brownies

Well– ...
... sh...
...p–p...

bodies!

1/2 C. butter
2 oz. chocolate } melt n cool
2 chocolate } sift together
3/4 C. flour
1/2 tsp. b. powder
1/2 tsp. salt
1/2 tsp. whi light

Beat 2 eggs whi light
Add sugar + chocolate mixture
1 tsp vanilla
... whole wn Beat sugar mixture
Add: flour mixture 8x8 @ 350° for 20-25 mins.
...e purpose Bake in greased 8x8 @ 350°
... use 1/2 ...

...y Herold's Brandy Beans

2 lbs. Sr beef
1 Sr onion
1 C. br. sugar
1/2 C. chili sauce
1 tsp. dry mustard
1/4 C. strong coffee
1/4 C. brandy or rum
6 reg. cans brown beans

Brown beef + onions

Add sugar, chili...
... stir ov
layer bea...
mixtu...
Top ε Ru...
Don't
Bake!

Recipe: Virginia's Meatballs

serves ____

2 # beef } ground
1 # pork } together
2 eggs – beaten
1/2 C. crumbs
salt, pepper, 1/4 tsp allspice
1/2 – 3/4 C. skim milk

Mix all together – roll into small balls – roll
in flour + brown – Add water or beef broth 1/2
barely cover   Cook slowly 1 1/2 hr.

from the kitchen of
75-924

...le's
...

meat
bread crumbs
cheese, velvetta.
chopped onion.
...ker}

...ing powder

Coleslaw
...

In My Mother's Kitchen

Ginny,
Enjoy these simple ideas!

In My
Mother's Kitchen

Three Generations of Simple, Delicious Family Food

TRISH MAGWOOD

PHOTOGRAPHY BY BRANDON BARRÉ

HarperCollins*Publishers*Ltd

Published by HarperCollins Publishers Ltd

First edition

HarperCollins Publishers Ltd.
2 Bloor Street East, 20th Floor
Toronto, Ontario, Canada
M4W 1A8

www.harpercollins.ca
www.trishmagwood.ca

Library and Archives Canada Cataloguing in Publication information is available

ISBN 978-1-44340-484-6

PP 9 8 7 6 5 4 3 2 1

Food by Trish Magwood with the help
of Lee Magwood and Elena Embrioni
Photos by Brandon Barré
Additional photography courtesy Trish Magwood
Styling by Trish Magwood

Mom
Happy Mother's Day
Love Kari

May, 2011

To Mom and Bo,

for teaching me the importance

of the gathering, to love good food,

to share it and to pass it on.

Contents

Introduction

For so many of us, our mother's kitchen is a place where memories and meals are shared. In her kitchen, my mother fed four hungry mouths with delicious, simple food. We always sat at the table to eat and we always had dessert (if we ate our dinner). Her kitchen was also where we carved pumpkins, pulled out first teeth, learned to tie shoes, cried over fights with friends and stuck together as a large and boisterous family over yummy food.

In both my grandmother Dodie's and grandmother Bo's kitchens, there was the same energy. Those kitchens were where Sunday and special-occasion dinners happened—kitchens filled with the aroma of roast beef and Yorkshire pudding. Today Bo's kitchen is still her focal point. It's where she lovingly prepares tomato butter and crabapple jelly every fall. And it's where our third child, Charlotte, visits mid-week mornings for freshly squeezed OJ and sticky buns with her great-aunt Nancy and great-grandmother Bo.

The family kitchen is the hub of our own home—kids' lunches and "fancy tea parties," Bryce's weekend eggs and as many meals together as possible. We are creating our own traditions and happy memories in the kitchen. These are fleeting moments, so we are trying to grab hold of them over simple meals. Our meals are not always a success. Findlay, Olivia and Charlotte are quick to let me know "this is not my favourite." With much trial and error, I have gathered a book's worth of family meals that are for the most part wild successes, even with Fin, our picky seven-year-old, and my grown-up brother Robbie, who is just as picky.

My new mantra: keep it simple and fresh, and focus on the gathering, even if the broccoli is left on the plate.

We all love gathering in other kitchens too. It is in these other kitchens—the kitchens of my grandmother Bo, my mom of course, my sisters-in-law Nancy, Amy and Amanda and my friends like Ghislaine, Liz and Tori—where family meal inspiration and shopping secrets come from, where recipes and ideas are shared and where the kids and adults love to gather. It's a broader definition of the family kitchen.

These are my people and places of inspiration and ideas for this collection of four generations' worth of simple, delicious meals that work. There's not a lot of fuss because there's not a lot of time. These meals bring the biggest smiles, allowing us to have a quick chat and hold on to the connections, because it all goes so fast.

Dish entertains, my first book, shared my favourite recipes for everyday simple and special-occasion gatherings, based on my work life at dish cooking studio and my TV show, *party dish*. *In My Mother's Kitchen* is life at home. It's a personal collection of family recipes and stories that I hope will bring ease, allowing you to celebrate connections in your kitchen.

Reflections on Food and Family

As I am fast approaching forty, a bunch of things are happening. I spend much time looking to friends, family, acquaintances and even strangers for ideas, sources and inspiration, sometimes for what to wear for a glam fundraiser, sometimes where to get inexpensive art for empty walls in an otherwise full home, but mostly for what on earth to buy and cook for kids' lunches and family dinners.

As our kids grow, as our parents age and as we ourselves gain wrinkles, we crave more and deeper connections. We look back and learn from family traditions so that we can create our own traditions and definitions of family. Our days are still organized around meals, but now, as we try to excel in our jobs and still be there for our kids, mealtime is more frantic and less enjoyable. But the need to connect and share with family and friends, even though life is busy, has not changed.

In this book, I have tried to bring tradition and old family recipes into the present day to help all of us, in the context of our busy lives, figure out how to enjoy a good meal. If we keep it simple (thirty minutes or less for mid-week), try to sit together when we can (or at

1939

least sit down with the kids while they eat), then we will all enjoy the meal, eat better and be happier for it. I have pulled together a collection of recipes that had to meet these criteria:

- no tears when it came to the table: all five of us, adults and kids, had to like it (or at least try it),
- it couldn't take me more than thirty minutes (except for the weekend slow roasts and some of the special-occasion dinners like turkey),
- it couldn't cost a fortune,
- it was as local, fresh and healthy as possible (the healthy part has a few exceptions, of course!), and
- it was one of the recipes I have loved or cooked for a long time, from my own old recipe book or from a recipe box from a friend or family member who was a really good cook—a recipe or idea from our collective mothers' kitchens.

My starting point for this book was my mother. She is a great cook. Though she's rigid about measuring and a real chicken about trying new things, especially new cultural inspirations, her recipes, ultimately collected from her own family and friends, are packed with flavour and are no-fail successes.

Then there was my father's garden. My parents are a bit like the Cleavers—my mom's domain is the kitchen, whereas my dad's domain is the outdoors. He is most happy in a ratty old coat, covered in mud from his cross-country ATV adventure, emerging from the bush smelling of fire and sap after his labours over a spring batch of old-school maple syrup. My dad doesn't do anything in a small way. Everything is with big expression. The vineyard has grown as far as the eye can see. (He's only four years in, so we have yet to try the home brew.) He and farmer Kate, the most patient and knowledgeable woman of the earth I know, spend their days grafting the apple trees and nurturing tomatoes and assortments of lettuces I have never heard of. It doesn't get any more local or organic. Findlay, our eldest, and the pickiest eater, is only ever caught eating green vegetables with my dad, straight from the garden with dirty hands, or with my mother, at a standoff at the table. So *In My Mother's Kitchen* would not be complete without adding "and from my father's garden." It is because of this garden that I have fallen back in love with food and have found the most basic of inspirations and ideas for salads and sides.

I realize how lucky I am coming from a family where Bo, my ninety-six-year-old grandmother, still reigns supreme in a kitchen where fresh-made ginger cookies and vegetable soup are a daily norm. My mom rises to the almost weekly occasion of cooking for twenty of us—that's just our core family—on the weekend. (That would put many a good cook over the edge.) My sisters-in-law seamlessly work their magic into my mom's meal plan—Amanda's master hostess hors d'oeuvres and baked goodies, Nancy's killer salads and Amy's ski lunch spreads. We all take our traditions, twist them and either never repeat the disasters or add the resounding successes to our repertoire, and now to this book.

I have often thought back to the first cookbook I did—not *dish entertains*, but a handwritten journal-style book for my great friends Sarah and Paul as they continued with their studies at Queen's while the rest of us left Kingston. They were my best recipes, ones we all cooked together: Lynnie's Wild Rice Salad, Kristi's Brandy Beans, Bay's Veggie Lasagna and my desserts, lots of desserts. The value of the recipes shared among friends is priceless. The gathering and sharing of recipes is more about helping to make one another's lives a bit easier and more enriched.

I am so happy to share with you this collection of my favourite simple, yummy family recipes from my kitchen, from my mother's and grandmother's and in-laws' and friends' kitchens and their mothers' kitchens. Pass them on, share, connect and enjoy.

Thanks

To Elena, my compadre, seasoned hardcore resto chef, friend and adopted entertainer for our kids, thank you for taking three days to get here from Argentina and spending a month in the heat of our house, cooking with love and humour and seasoned taste buds.

To Brandon, the man of few words and extraordinary pictures. Thank you for sharing my vision, for creating beautiful photos and for patiently spending countless hours with my family.

To Mom, for your precision and dedication to every detail in every recipe. You are details, I am big picture, and together we make a great team. You take care of people through your love of food and family, and your strength and optimism could lead a country.

To Dad, for your Martha Stewart–style produce deliveries, for your endless garden supplies and for your boundless energy and enthusiasm and love for the land and family.

To Bo, my source of inspiration. If only I could love to cook as much as you, and if only I could have a bit of your wisdom and stories. Thank you for setting the example of what it means to be a vibrant, youthful, interested family matriarch, and thank you for my lifetime of yummy meals and happy times. Tim, Jeff, Robbie and I, along with Nancy, Amy, Amanda and Bryce and our gaggle of kids—Fin, Olivia, Charlotte, Ryan, Sophie, Zac, Signy, Gavin and Paige—are so very lucky.

To Bryce, the consummate calm, patient ship who keeps us all on course, no matter how much I rock the boat. Thank you for eating the less-than-delicious experiments and for cheerleading me to do this second book. And to your family—Judi, Lionel, Duff, Lionel, Joannie, Chas, Chloe and Jasper—for sharing in the love of family. To Findlay, Olivia and Charlotte, for being brave and trying new things, for understanding how important good food is and for your honesty and laughs. You will always get dessert if you eat your dinner.

To my testers, the women whom I call my friends and who can really cook. To the cooks I trust and respect, thank you for fixing my mistakes, for sharing your knowledge and passion for cooking and for being a vital part of this book: Martha Mansfield, Stewie Baldwin, Kara Macintosh, Lee Magwood, Roberta Turner, Nancy Bowes, Kristi Herold, Elena Embrioni and Amanda Magwood. To Cory, for keeping us all laughing and beautiful, and to Lilana for keeping me busy.

To my HarperCollins dream team—my editor, Kirsten, who made this process enjoyable, and made me realize I had another book in me, and to our art director, Alan, for bringing my vision to life and making it all seem so easy.

To my contributors and friends, thank you for being proud cooks. Thank you for sharing your favourite recipes and for spending time with me with sharing your stories and yummy ideas. To the cooks in our family: Amanda, Nancy, Amy, Judi, Nancy, Bo, Dawn and Mom. My dear friends Elena, Tori, Kara, Christie, Kristi, Ghislaine, Rahat, Liz, Lynn, Foofie, Paula, Rebecca, Jen, Shannon, Robin, Lisa, Karen, Derek, Ron, Mike, Sarah, Tori N., Patsy, Jane and Janet. To Mom's, Nancy's and Judi's friends and my friends' moms, the generation of food wisdom: farmer Kate, Stewie, Mrs. Wendy, Mrs. Harry, Bonnie, Ebie, Bibby, Judi B., Anne D., Daphne, Mary, Louise, Pam, Lynn, Lionel, Kathy, Mardi and Bernie. And to Bo and Dodie's generation, Helen and Auntie Mary, who truly wrote the book of good food. And to all those Pointe au Baril women who put together my favourite cookbook, *The Cottage Cookbook*, thank you for sharing your favourites and for allowing me to share your secrets.

What I have learned over the years of recipe collecting, testing, writing, teaching, cooking and eating is that there is a massive interconnectedness in food. We inspire, teach and help one another, challenge and make changes, and then create things we call our own. There is a familiarity in good old recipes that show up, in different forms and versions, time and time again. They spark a discussion or at least a comment, or even friendly competition—"that's my mom's cheese dip recipe from Winnipeg," a similar dip found in Sudbury and another on the shores of Georgian Bay. In this age of endless information and constant change, a few things have remained the same—we all long for a piece of our past, we all crave good food and we all want simple, quick recipes, and the tips and tricks that go along with them, so we can sit for a moment at the end of the day and enjoy a meal with family, in some variation, even for a moment, and say, "That was good. Thank you!"

Breakfasts

Smoothies

When berries are in season, I stock up and freeze them so I have local berries on hand for quickie breakfast smoothies, even in winter. These recipes are guidelines—use whatever fruit you have on hand. Charlotte, Olivia and Findlay prefer the milky smoothies, whereas Bryce and I prefer the juice smoothies.

Strawberry Banana Milky Smoothies

MAKES 4 SMOOTHIES

INGREDIENTS

1 cup (250 mL) frozen strawberries

3 bananas

1 cup (250 mL) plain yogurt

1 cup (250 mL) milk

1 tbsp (15 mL) maple syrup

1 tsp (5 mL) flax oil

HOW TO

Place strawberries, bananas, yogurt, milk and maple syrup in a blender and purée on high until smooth. Add flax oil and give one more quick purée.

Mixed Berry Juice Smoothies

MAKES 4 SMOOTHIES

INGREDIENTS

1 1/2 cups (375 mL) frozen mixed berries

3 bananas

1 cup (250 mL) vanilla yogurt

1 cup (250 mL) cranberry juice or fresh orange juice

1 tsp (5 mL) flax oil

HOW TO

Place berries, bananas, yogurt and juice in a blender and purée on high until smooth. Add flax oil and give one more quick purée.

Kitchen Notes: To freeze fresh berries, spread in one layer on a baking sheet and freeze until hardened, about 1 hour. Once frozen, put them into resealable plastic bags.
If you use fresh fruit, add 1 1/2 cups (375 mL) crushed ice to give you the right consistency.
Flax oil is a healthy source of good fatty acids. It does not change the flavour of the smoothie.

Apricot and Cranberry Buttermilk Scones

For almost ten years, these scones were a favourite dish café item. Former dish chef Elena popularized them, and she still makes the best!

MAKES 8 MEDIUM SCONES

INGREDIENTS

3 cups (750 mL) all-purpose flour

1/3 cup (75 mL) sugar

2 1/2 tsp (12 mL) baking powder

1/2 tsp (2 mL) baking soda

3/4 tsp (4 mL) salt

3/4 cup (175 mL) cold butter, cubed

1/2 cup (125 mL) chopped dried apricots

1/2 cup (125 mL) dried cranberries

1 cup (250 mL) buttermilk, plus 1 tbsp
   (15 mL) for brushing

1/4 cup (60 mL) rock sugar, for dusting

HOW TO

Preheat oven to 375°F (190°C). Line a cookie sheet with parchment paper.

In the bowl of a food processor, combine flour, sugar, baking powder, baking soda and salt. Add butter and pulse just until mixture resembles coarse meal, leaving a few pea-sized pieces of butter. (You can also do this in a bowl, using a pastry blender.)

Pour into a bowl. Using a fork, stir in apricots and cranberries until mixed throughout. Stir in buttermilk just until incorporated. Do not over-mix.

Gather dough into a ball until it just holds together. Transfer dough to a floured surface and knead briefly. Press into a circle about 3/4 inch (2 cm) thick. Cut into 8 triangles. Transfer triangles to prepared cookie sheet. Brush tops with remaining 1 tbsp (15 mL) buttermilk and sprinkle with rock sugar.

Bake for 20 minutes or until golden. Serve warm.

....

Kitchen Notes: As with pastry, you don't want to overwork the batter. Mix until liquid is just incorporated to keep scones light and fluffy.

You can bake these halfway, cool, freeze and bake from frozen for 10 minutes—what a treat to have these on hand in the freezer!

You can make 12 small scones and bake them for 15 minutes.

Variations: Substitute other dried fruits or nuts (macadamias are delicious) or lemon zest and juice.

Cheddar Chive Buttermilk Scones

These scones were a big hit at the café at dish. Visitors would call ahead to make sure some were left. I loved the savoury taste—it made a refreshing change from sweet morning-baked goodies.

MAKES 8 MEDIUM SCONES

INGREDIENTS

3 cups (750 mL) all-purpose flour

2 1/2 tsp (12 mL) baking powder

1/2 tsp (2 mL) baking soda

3/4 tsp (4 mL) salt

3/4 cup (175 mL) cold butter, cubed

2 cups (500 mL) grated extra-old white
   Cheddar cheese

1/4 cup (60 mL) finely chopped chives

1 cup (250 mL) buttermilk, plus 1 tbsp
   (15 mL) for brushing

Flaky sea salt, for topping

HOW TO

Preheat oven to 375°F (190°C). Line a cookie sheet with parchment paper.

In the bowl of a food processor, combine flour, baking powder, baking soda and salt. Add butter and pulse just until mixture resembles coarse meal, leaving a few pea-sized pieces of butter. (You can also do this in a bowl, using a pastry blender.)

Pour into a bowl. Using a fork, stir in cheese and chives until mixed throughout. Stir in buttermilk just until incorporated. Do not over-mix.

Gather dough into a ball until it just holds together. Transfer dough to a floured surface and knead briefly. Press into a circle about 3/4 inch (2 cm) thick. Cut into 8 triangles. Transfer triangles to prepared cookie sheet. Brush tops with remaining 1 tbsp (15 mL) buttermilk and sprinkle with sea salt.

Bake for 20 to 25 minutes or until golden. Serve warm.

....

Kitchen Notes: You can bake these halfway, cool, freeze and bake from frozen for 10 to 12 minutes. You can make 12 small scones and bake them for 15 minutes.

Buttermilk: Add this to your fridge staples. It used to be the liquid remaining after butter was churned, but now they simply add bacteria to low-fat milk to give a thick, tangy, low-fat liquid that's great to use in scones, banana bread, chocolate cake and soups.

Variation: For an almond variation, replace the buttermilk with almond milk and add 1/4 cup (60 mL) slivered toasted almonds.

Banana Bread

This is a great snack to fill up the picky eater with good-for-you bananas. The buttermilk keeps the fat content in check and keeps the bread super-moist. The kids love this loaf as a team soccer snack or breakfast on the go, and I love it for coffee visits. **MAKES 2 LOAVES**

INGREDIENTS

3 cups (750 mL) all-purpose flour

2 tsp (10 mL) baking soda

2 tsp (10 mL) baking powder

1/2 tsp (2 mL) cinnamon

1/2 tsp (2 mL) salt

4 large eggs, at room temperature

1 1/2 cups (375 mL) brown sugar

3/4 cup (175 mL) vegetable oil

3 cups (750 mL) mashed very ripe bananas (6 large)

1/2 cup (125 mL) buttermilk

2 tsp (10 mL) vanilla

1 cup (250 mL) chocolate chips (optional)

HOW TO

Preheat oven to 350°F (180°C). Butter and flour two 9- x 5-inch (2 L) loaf pans.

In a bowl, sift together flour, baking soda, baking powder, cinnamon and salt.

In a large bowl, with an electric mixer, beat eggs with sugar at medium-high speed until mixture is very thick, pale and forms a ribbon when beater is lifted, about 10 minutes. Reduce speed to low and add oil in a slow stream.

Stir in bananas, buttermilk and vanilla. Fold in flour mixture and chocolate chips, if using. Divide batter between loaf pans, spreading evenly.

Bake for 60 minutes or until light brown and a toothpick inserted into the centre comes out clean.

Cool loaves in pans on rack for 10 minutes, then turn out onto rack. Turn loaves right side up and cool completely.

....

Kitchen Notes: This banana bread freezes well—wrap first in plastic wrap, then in foil.
The chocolate chips are a great way to get the kids to eat bananas. You can also substitute chopped toasted walnuts.

Bran Muffins in a Pail

Bake fresh muffins on the fly with ready-made batter. When I first found this recipe—it's from my grandmother Bo's church group—I was heading off to Red Lake, Ontario, to cook for fifty hungry workers at a tree-planting camp. This recipe is perfect for a healthy breakfast packed with good stuff (and good for a crowd). I've cut the recipe down, as I'm sure you don't need muffins for fifty. Still, since the batter lasts in the fridge for six weeks (that's not a typo), if you double or triple the recipe, you can make muffins in an instant should fifty people drop by.

MAKES ENOUGH BATTER FOR 24 LARGE MUFFINS

INGREDIENTS

2 1/2 tsp (12 mL) baking soda

1 cup (250 mL) boiling water

1/2 cup (125 mL) butter

1 cup (250 mL) sugar

2 eggs

2 cups (500 mL) buttermilk

2 1/2 cups (625 mL) all-purpose flour

1 1/2 tsp (7 mL) salt

2 cups (500 mL) 100% bran cereal

1 1/2 cups (375 mL) natural wheat bran

1 cup (250 mL) chopped, pitted honey dates

1/2 cup (125 mL) raisins

HOW TO

Stir baking soda into boiling water and let cool.

In your largest bowl, cream butter with sugar until light and fluffy. Add eggs and beat well. Stir in buttermilk. Stir in flour and salt. Stir in soda/water mixture.

In a separate bowl, combine bran cereal, wheat bran, dates and raisins. Stir into wet mixture. Batter can be stored in a tightly sealed container in the fridge for up to 6 weeks.

To bake muffins, fill desired number of greased or paper-lined muffin cups two-thirds full. Bake in a 400°F (200°C) oven for 20 to 25 minutes or until a toothpick inserted in the centre comes out clean.

....

Kitchen Notes: Make sure to mark the date on container so you know your best-before date. It's worth buying good-quality dates—premium dates make all the difference. I love pitted honey dates.

Cornmeal Jammy Muffins

These muffins were inspired by a recipe in Ina Garten's *The Barefoot Contessa Cookbook*. Incorporating my aunt's friend Daphne's subtle changes in her signature entertaining go-to, these muffins will surely make your favourites list. Go ahead and experiment to come up with your own version for brunch or lunch as a tasty alternative to bread.

MAKES 6 TO 8 MUFFINS

INGREDIENTS

2 cups (500 mL) all-purpose flour

1 1/4 cups (300 mL) medium cornmeal

1/2 cup (125 mL) sugar

1 tbsp (15 mL) baking powder

3/4 tsp (4 mL) salt

2 large eggs

1 cup (250 mL) milk

3/4 cup (175 mL) butter, melted and cooled

1/4 cup (60 mL) maple syrup

1/2 cup (125 mL) fruit preserves or good-quality jam

HOW TO

Preheat oven to 375°F (190°C). Grease 6 to 8 cups of a muffin pan or line with paper liners.

In a large bowl, combine flour, cornmeal, sugar, baking powder and salt.

In a separate bowl, lightly beat eggs. Stir in milk, melted butter and maple syrup. Add to dry ingredients, stirring just until combined. The batter will be a bit lumpy. Using a large ice cream scoop, fill muffin cups about two-thirds full.

Bake for 20 to 22 minutes or until light brown and a toothpick inserted in the centre comes out clean. Cool on rack.

When muffins are cool, make a small well in the top of each one and spoon in the preserves or jam.

....

Kitchen Notes: Use medium cornmeal—it gives the muffins a more coarse cornmeal texture than the more common fine cornmeal. It's a bit tricky to find but worth the hunt. A health food store or specialty food shop should carry it.

Variation: Replace the jam topping with a fresh blackberry or raspberry.

Lemon Poppy Seed Muffins

I got hooked on Starbucks' lemon poppy seed loaf after my workouts, which unfortunately completely defeated the purpose of the exercise. And so began my hunt for a slightly healthier lemon poppy seed creation, which ended with this recipe. To revert to a less healthy but equally delicious version, add some cream cheese to the glaze and ice the cooled muffins.

MAKES 12 MUFFINS

INGREDIENTS

2 cups (500 mL) all-purpose flour

1 tsp (5 mL) baking soda

1 tsp (5 mL) baking powder

1/2 tsp (2 mL) salt

1/4 cup (60 mL) poppy seeds

3/4 cup (175 mL) butter, softened

1 cup (250 mL) sugar

2 eggs

1 cup (250 mL) buttermilk

1/4 cup (60 mL) plain yogurt

Zest and juice of 2 lemons (about 1/2 cup/125 mL juice)

GLAZE

Juice of 1 lemon

1/3 cup (75 mL) icing sugar

HOW TO

Preheat oven to 375°F (190°C). Line a muffin pan with paper liners.

Sift together flour, baking soda, baking powder and salt. Stir in poppy seeds.

In a separate bowl, using an electric mixer, cream butter with sugar until fluffy. Add eggs one at a time, beating well after each addition. Beat until pale yellow, scraping down the sides of the bowl.

In a measuring cup, mix buttermilk, yogurt, lemon zest and lemon juice.

Add half the dry mixture to the batter, then half the buttermilk mixture. Repeat, stirring until just incorporated. Do not over-mix. Using an ice cream scoop or 1/3-cup (75 mL) measure, fill muffin cups three-quarters full.

Bake for 15 to 20 minutes or until a toothpick inserted in the centre comes out clean. Let stand 10 minutes.

To make the glaze, drizzle lemon juice into icing sugar until mixture is runny. Using a skewer, poke a few holes in the top of each warm muffin and pour glaze over.

Family Granola

When I held a competition for the "best" granola, so many people contributed great recipes that I just couldn't make up my mind. This recipe combines the best of my age-old granola and my friends Kara's and Ebie's versions. My seasoned recipe tester Chef Elena Embrioni stepped in with her final tweaks.

MAKES 12 CUPS (3 L)

INGREDIENTS

4 cups (1 L) quick-cooking rolled oats

2 cups (500 mL) sweetened shredded coconut

2 cups (500 mL) slivered almonds, chopped

1 tsp (5 mL) cinnamon

1/2 cup (125 mL) vegetable oil

1/2 cup (125 mL) maple syrup

1/4 cup (60 mL) honey

1 cup (250 mL) dried cranberries

1 cup (250 mL) golden raisins or dried cherries

1 cup (250 mL) chopped dried apples or mangoes

1 cup (250 mL) chopped dried apricots

1/2 cup (125 mL) sunflower seeds

1/2 cup (125 mL) chopped cashews

1/4 cup (60 mL) flax seeds

HOW TO

Preheat oven to 325°F (160°C). Line a large baking sheet with foil; lightly oil the foil.

In a large bowl, combine oats, coconut, almonds and cinnamon. In a separate bowl, combine oil, maple syrup and honey; gently fold into dry mixture until coated, allowing clumps to form. Spread mixture evenly on the baking sheet.

Bake for 30 minutes, stirring occasionally, or until light golden brown. Remove from oven, stir again and cool. Stir in dried fruits, nuts and seeds.

Store in an airtight container. Granola keeps 2 weeks at room temperature (if you can keep it around that long!).

....

Kitchen Notes: This is the perfect breakfast with fresh berries and your favourite yogurt. It's also an ideal car or stroller snack. I even sometimes have this as dinner or a late-night snack.

Variations: Add pumpkin seeds or sesame seeds, wheat germ or bran.

Eggs Every Way You Like Them

At chef school in New York we spent days on eggs. The first thing I was tested on was a scrambled egg, and I was terrified. But, as Julia Child confidently explained, cooking is household science and requires practice, practice, practice! So with a little study and lots of practice I was just fine—and I am no longer afraid of the humble egg.

Egg in a Hole

My mom used to make these for us when we were kids—we loved "breakfast for dinner." Alongside, serve up bacon or sausages with maple syrup for dipping, and salsa or roasted tomatoes for the eggs. Fry the cut-out circles as well, and serve alongside.

SERVES 4

INGREDIENTS

4 slices whole grain bread

4 tsp (20 mL) butter

4 eggs

Salt and pepper to taste

1 tsp (5 mL) chopped chives, for garnish

HOW TO

Use a 2-inch (5 cm) cookie cutter to cut a hole from the middle of each slice of bread.

In a large frying pan, melt butter over medium heat. Put bread in pan and turn to coat with butter. Cook bread 1 minute each side. Crack an egg into each hole and fry 1 to 2 minutes, until the eggs are set. Flip and fry 1 more minute or until cooked to your liking. Season with salt and pepper and garnish with chives.

Soft-Boiled "Grandie Eggs" with Soldier Fingers

Bryce's mom, Judi, used to have soft-boiled eggs almost every morning at the cottage. The kids love them with "soldier fingers," and we dubbed them "Grandie Eggs." A favourite egg cup is key for enjoyment.

HOW TO

Judi says once the water starts to boil, put the toast on—that's how long it takes. Loosely translated:

Put eggs in a small saucepan. Cover with cold water. Bring to boil over high heat. As soon as the water hits the boil, put the toast on. Lower heat to a simmer and cook eggs 3 minutes. Butter toast and slice lengthwise into strips. Put each egg in an egg cup, crack the top off, sprinkle with salt and pepper, and dip with toast.

Poached Eggs

Making poached eggs can be intimidating at first. It's more of a science than an art, so like most things in school, practice makes perfect.

SERVES 4

INGREDIENTS
6 cups (1.5 L) water
1/4 cup (60 mL) white vinegar
4 eggs

HOW TO
Bring water and vinegar to a bare simmer in a large saucepan.

Crack 1 egg into a small bowl. Whisk water vigorously to create a whirlpool. Carefully pour egg into water. Repeat with remaining eggs.

Keeping water at a gentle simmer with just a few bubbles, cook for 4 to 5 minutes or until eggs leave the bottom of the pan and rise to the surface.

Kitchen Notes: Serve poached eggs on potato pancakes or with your favourite toast. Garnish with chopped parsley and serve with warm wilted baby spinach.

Scrambled Eggs

There's something comforting about the simplicity of eggs for dinner. Our kids "order" scrambled eggs on the weekend—a great way to start the day.

SERVES 2

INGREDIENTS
4 eggs
2 tsp (10 mL) milk

Pinch each salt and pepper
1 tsp (5 mL) butter

HOW TO
In a small bowl, lightly whisk together eggs, milk and salt and pepper until completely combined.

Heat a 7- or 8-inch (18 to 20 cm) nonstick frying pan over medium heat. Add butter and heat until foamy but not brown. Pour in egg mixture. When eggs begin to set around edges, shake pan lightly and, using a spatula, gently push eggs across the pan back and forth. Cook until eggs are almost set but still moist, about 1 minute.

Kitchen Notes: You need a small heavy nonstick pan. A good pan makes all the difference. Eggs are about the only thing I use a nonstick pan for. Nonstick is perfect for quickly cooking eggs, but for nearly everything else I want the sticky bits in the bottom of the pan for a sauce.

Make sure the pan is good and hot before the eggs go in, so they cook quickly and end up fluffy, not rubbery.

Don't overcook your eggs. They're done pretty quickly, so don't leave your post—don't answer the phone or check your email!

Remove the eggs from the pan when they are still a bit moist. They will continue to cook even out of the pan.

Simple Omelette for One

How often have you been at home with an empty fridge? Chances are you have eggs, though. A simple omelette makes the perfect meal when you don't feel like doing much cooking. There are two ways to make an omelette: my mom's way—small and simple with just one or two fillings—or Bryce's way—massive and stuffed with every imaginable cheese and vegetable. Whichever you choose, prepare your fillings before you start—the eggs don't take long to cook.

SERVES 1

INGREDIENTS

2 eggs

2 tsp (10 mL) milk

Pinch each salt and pepper

1 tsp (5 mL) butter

2 tbsp (30 mL) diced vegetables
and/or meat (see Fillings, below, for ideas)

2 tbsp (30 mL) grated or crumbled cheese

HOW TO

In a small bowl, lightly whisk together eggs, milk and salt and pepper until completely combined. Heat a 7- to 8-inch (18 to 20 cm) nonstick frying pan over medium heat. Add butter and heat until foamy but not brown. Pour in egg mixture. When eggs begin to set around edges, shake pan lightly and, using a spatula, gently push eggs from edges to centre, without stirring, so the uncooked portion flows underneath. Cook until eggs are almost set but still moist, about 1 minute. Spoon veggie and/or meat fillings across the centre and cook for another 30 seconds, or until the underside is light golden. Sprinkle filling with cheese. Fold one side of omelette over filling, then roll once in the same direction to close. Tilt pan and slip omelette onto a plate.

Fillings

Red onion, finely chopped

Sweet red pepper, finely chopped

Button mushrooms, finely chopped

Chives or other fresh herbs, chopped

Spinach, chopped

Asparagus, chopped

Tomatoes, seeded and diced

Cheeses—chèvre, Cheddar, Gorgonzola,
Gruyère

Meats—bacon, ham

Salsa

Or whatever else you have in the fridge!

Ebie's Huevos Rancheros

My mom's friend Ebie sent me this simple recipe, which was an instant hit in our house. I love the all-in-one-pan, little-morning-mess brekkie solution. **SERVES 2 TO 4**

INGREDIENTS

3 tbsp (50 mL) butter

1 medium onion, chopped

1/2 sweet green pepper, julienned

4 tomatoes, chopped

1 1/2 tsp (7 mL) chili powder

1/4 tsp (1 mL) salt

1 clove garlic, crushed

2 tbsp (30 mL) tomato paste

4 eggs

3/4 cup (175 mL) grated aged Cheddar
   or Monterey Jack cheese

Paprika

HOW TO

Preheat oven to 450°F (230°C).

In a medium ovenproof frying pan, melt butter over medium-high heat. Add onion and sauté 5 minutes or until soft. Add green peppers and sauté another 2 minutes or until tender. Stir in tomatoes, chili powder, salt, garlic and tomato paste; cook for 20 minutes or until tomatoes are reduced.

Make four holes in the sauce and break eggs into them. Cover with cheese; sprinkle with paprika. Bake, uncovered, until egg whites are set, 10 to 15 minutes.

Raisin Walnut French Toast with 4 Wheel Farm Maple Syrup

I'm pretty sure this is my favourite breakfast! My dad's maple syrup makes it the best.

SERVES 4

INGREDIENTS

1 loaf raisin walnut bread
6 eggs
1 cup (250 mL) whole milk
2 tsp (10 mL) vanilla
1/2 tsp (2 mL) cinnamon
1/4 tsp (1 mL) salt
2 tsp (10 mL) butter
1/2 cup (125 mL) maple syrup, hot
1/2 cup (125 mL) plain yogurt
1 pint (500 mL) fresh raspberries, for garnish

HOW TO

Preheat oven to 200°F (100°C).

Cut bread into 1/2-inch (1 cm) slices. In a shallow bowl, whisk together eggs, milk, vanilla, cinnamon and salt.

In a large frying pan, melt butter over medium heat. Dip bread into egg mixture, turning to coat completely. Cook slices, a few at a time and leaving room around each piece, about 2 minutes, turning once. Keep warm in a single layer on a baking sheet in the oven while you repeat with remaining bread.

Transfer French toast to a warm platter. Pour hot maple syrup over and dollop a little yogurt on each piece. Garnish with raspberries.

....

Variation: This is also delicious made with hallah bread.

Oven-Baked French Toast

This is a delicious make-ahead if you are having friends over for Sunday breakfast or want to be prepared the night before for a birthday breakfast—a tradition in our house.

SERVES 6 TO 8

INGREDIENTS

7 eggs

2 1/4 cups (550 mL) milk

2 tsp (10 mL) cinnamon

Pinch salt

12 to 18 slices (1 inch/2.5 cm thick) day-old brioche or hallah loaf, crusts removed
    (2 to 3 loaves)

1/2 cup (125 mL) butter, melted

1/2 cup (125 mL) brown sugar

HOW TO

Lightly butter a 9- x 13-inch (3 L) baking pan.

In a medium bowl, whisk together eggs, milk, cinnamon and salt. Dip bread in egg mixture, turning
    to coat both sides. Arrange in layers in prepared pan. Pour remaining egg mixture over top. Stir
    together butter and brown sugar and drizzle over top. Cover with foil and refrigerate overnight.
    Bring to room temperature before baking.

Preheat oven to 400°F (200°C). Remove foil and bake for 30 to 35 minutes or until top is golden
    and custard has set.

Serve with maple syrup, fresh fruit and a dollop of yogurt.

Perfect Coffee Two Ways

Old-Fashioned Percolated Coffee

"Perc" coffee is my favourite. The aroma reminds me of my grandparents' place, or waking up at my parents' home. This is the way my aunt Nancy makes her coffee every morning. (Since it's so good, I try to show up at her house just at coffee time!) My mom, Lee, makes coffee the same way at the cottage. There is a sticky note on the wall with very specific instructions (such as the seven-minute boil).

INGREDIENTS

1/2 lb (250 g) freshly roasted dark roast coffee beans
Cold water

HOW TO

Grind beans on coarse grind. For each cup of coffee, use 1 generous spoonful (20 mL) of freshly ground coffee and 1 cup (250 mL) cold water.

Place percolator on medium heat for a glass pot (or medium-high for metal). When the water starts to perk through the top, turn heat down to low so you still see a gentle perc. When the water becomes dark—after 7 minutes—turn off the heat.

Pour a splash of cold water into the spout to settle the grounds. Pour a mug, step outside and enjoy. Best in pyjamas outdoors with family early in the morning.

Kitchen Notes: Percolated coffee is always the hottest, because electric coffee makers don't bring water to a full boil. You will need a good old-fashioned percolator—glass is the best, as it does not impart any metallic taste.
Don't keep your ground coffee longer than a week.

Steeped Coffee

This is Derek Zavislake's preferred home method. Derek's business is coffee; he owns Merchants of Green Coffee in Toronto. So he should know!

HOW TO

Add cold fresh water to kettle and bring to a boil.

Grind freshly roasted coffee beans in a burr grinder to medium grind.

Place 10 g (1 tbsp/15 mL) ground coffee per cup of coffee in a steeping pot.

Add 1/2 cup (125 mL) boiling water per cup of coffee. Steep for 2 to 3 minutes. Break the crust on the top by swirling the pot. Then pour the water and coffee grinds through a filter, such as a cloth or gold filter, and into a decanter or thermos.

Taste. If it is too strong, add more boiled water to desired strength. If it is too weak, you'll have to start over, so err on the side of strong!

Enjoy immediately!

Derek's Coffee Tips

Adherence to the "three keys" is the only way to enjoy coffee at its peak, according to Derek:

Quality arabica green beans—the best beans produce the best cup of coffee.

Freshly roasted beans—freshly roasted coffee must be consumed within 5 days (for whole beans), 4 hours (ground coffee) or 15 minutes (brewed coffee).

Proper brewing—water just below the boil (195 to 205°F/90 to 96°C) and good coffee-to-water contact produce the best cup of coffee.

Soups

Summer Red Pepper Soup

Carrot Soup in a Mug

Creamy Winter Tomato Soup

Farm-Fresh Tomato Soup with Basil

Sweet Potato Soup

Mrs. Chiviero's Stracciatella

Elena's Curried Corn Chowder

Mulligatawny Soup

Bibby's Taco Soup

Grannie Annie's Magic Soup

Homemade Chicken Stock

Summer Red Pepper Soup

A variation of this soup is in my first book, *dish entertains*. This version is even simpler and is a summer soup ritual of my mother-in-law's. Judi always has a batch in the fridge—it's a perfect cottage lunch and great for impromptu drop-ins.

SERVES 6 TO 8

INGREDIENTS

1/3 cup (75 mL) butter

2 cups (500 mL) chopped leeks (2 large, white part only)

4 cups (1 L) chopped sweet red peppers (4 medium)

1 1/2 cups (375 mL) chicken stock

4 cups (1 L) buttermilk

Chopped chives or basil, for garnish

HOW TO

In a large soup pot, melt butter over medium heat. Add leeks and cook, stirring occasionally, for 5 minutes or until translucent. Add peppers and cook for 10 minutes. Add chicken stock and simmer, uncovered, for 30 minutes.

Remove from heat. Using a hand blender, purée until smooth. (Or, using a blender, purée in batches.) Add buttermilk and stir well. Chill. Serve garnished with chives or basil.

....

Kitchen Notes: Keep in a pretty pitcher in the fridge and enjoy with crusty breads and your favourite cheeses. When it's chilly out, warm this soup—it's great both ways. Serve with a dollop of sour cream or yogurt.

1 large pepper yields 1 cup (250 mL) chopped pepper, and 1 large leek yields 1 cup (250 mL) chopped leeks.

Carrot Soup in a Mug

This is the first soup I remember making. The original recipe came from my mom's friend Lynn Pady. Not only is it delicious, it's quick and easy, the kids like it and I always have the ingredients on hand.

SERVES 4

INGREDIENTS

1 tbsp (15 mL) butter
1 onion, chopped
1 lb (500 g) carrots, chopped (3 cups/750 mL)
3 cups (750 mL) low-sodium chicken stock
1 can (370 mL) evaporated milk
Salt and pepper
1 tbsp (15 mL) chopped parsley, for garnish

HOW TO

In a large heavy soup pot, melt butter over medium heat. Add onion and cook, stirring frequently, until soft, about 3 minutes. Add carrots and cook another 5 minutes. Add chicken stock and bring to a boil. Cover, reduce heat and simmer until carrots are soft, about 20 minutes.

Remove from heat. Using a hand blender, purée until very smooth. Stir in evaporated milk. Season to taste. Serve garnished with parsley.

....

Kitchen Notes: Put the pot in the sink before you purée, to prevent a mess.
This recipe doubles well.

Creamy Winter Tomato Soup

This pantry soup is so quick and so comforting, but tastes like it took you hours. It's also good cold.

SERVES 4 TO 6

INGREDIENTS

2 cans (each 28 oz/796 mL) chopped
tomatoes

2 roasted sweet red peppers, seeded

1/4 cup (60 mL) vegetable stock

2 tbsp (30 mL) sugar

Salt and black pepper to taste

1/4 cup (60 mL) 35% cream

3 tbsp (50 mL) butter, cubed

1 tbsp (15 mL) chopped fresh basil,
for garnish

HOW TO

In a food processor, purée tomatoes and red peppers. Pour into a saucepan and add stock, sugar and salt and pepper. Bring to a boil. Reduce heat and simmer for 15 to 20 minutes, until slightly thickened.

Stir in cream. Remove from heat and gradually whisk in butter, a piece at a time. Serve garnished with basil.

....

Kitchen Notes: Red peppers can be grilled whole directly on your cooktop gas flame or on a baking sheet under the broiler. Keep turning them until they're blackened all over, then remove stem and seeds. Seal in a plastic bag. When they're cool, peel off the charred skin. You can also use store-bought roasted red peppers.

Farm-Fresh Tomato Soup with Basil

This classic summer soup is liquid gold in the hot months when tomatoes and basil are at their prime. There are so many variations on this soup. This yummy one came from Doug Biggar.

SERVES 4 TO 6

INGREDIENTS

3 tbsp (50 mL) butter

1 large onion, chopped

1 medium carrot, shredded

4 large ripe tomatoes, peeled and cut into
chunks (about 4 cups/1 L)

1/2 cup (125 mL) packed fresh basil leaves

1 tbsp (15 mL) sugar

Salt and pepper to taste

3 cups (750 mL) good-quality vegetable or
chicken stock

Chopped chives or parsley, for garnish

HOW TO

In a 3-quart (3 L) saucepan, melt butter over medium heat. Add onion and carrot; cook, stirring, until onion is soft, about 10 minutes.

Stir in tomatoes, basil, sugar, salt and pepper and stock. Bring to a boil, stirring constantly. Reduce heat, cover and simmer for 10 minutes.

Using a hand blender, purée until smooth. Serve garnished with fresh herbs.

Kitchen Notes: You can substitute water for the stock.

Sweet Potato Soup

This comforting soup will make you realize just how easy making soup can be. You can quickly turn it into a squash soup by swapping squash for sweet potato. This soup is the easiest way for me to ensure my littlest one, Charlotte, is getting her veggies—babies love to slurp warm soup.

SERVES 6 TO 8

INGREDIENTS

1 tbsp (15 mL) vegetable oil

1 medium onion, chopped

2 cloves garlic, minced

1 tsp (5 mL) chopped fresh thyme (or 1/2 tsp/2 mL dried)

Salt and pepper to taste

3 large sweet potatoes, peeled and chopped

5 cups (1.25 L) chicken stock

2 green onions, for garnish

2 tbsp (30 mL) sour cream or 35% cream, for garnish

HOW TO

In a large soup pot, heat oil over medium-high heat. Sauté onion for 5 minutes or until soft. Add garlic and thyme and sauté another minute. Season with salt and pepper. Add sweet potatoes and stir to coat. Add stock and bring to a boil. Reduce heat, cover and simmer 20 minutes or until sweet potatoes are tender.

Meanwhile, cut green onions crosswise into thirds, then lengthwise into thin strips. Place in a bowl of cold water so they curl.

Remove soup from heat. Using a hand blender, purée until smooth. Taste, and adjust seasoning. Serve garnished with green onion curls and a dollop of sour cream or a swirl of cream.

Mrs. Chiviero's Stracciatella

When I first tested this recipe, the soup went cloudy and I wasn't getting the stringy egg texture I was looking for . . . but it still tasted delicious. I called Mrs. Chiviero's daughter Janet, who had given me the recipe, to get the magic-touch answer, and she called her cousin in Italy. Of course, as with other egg-based dishes, you have to be delicate with the temperature and not have it too hot. These old family recipes were all about feel and approximations, not precise measurements, so it took some time for me to actually create a recipe with amounts.

SERVES 6

INGREDIENTS

6 cups (1.5 L) good-quality chicken stock
1/4 tsp (1 mL) salt
1/4 tsp (1 mL) pepper
4 eggs, beaten
1 cup (250 mL) grated Parmigiano-Reggiano
2 tbsp (30 mL) chopped parsley

HOW TO

In a medium heavy pot, heat stock, salt and pepper over medium heat until simmering. Reduce heat to low. (If the stock is too hot, the eggs will curdle and the soup will go cloudy.)

Stirring constantly, add beaten eggs in a slow, steady stream and cook, stirring, until thin strands of egg form, about 1 minute.

Remove from heat. Stir in Parmigiano and parsley. Season with salt and pepper.

Serve immediately with a warm, crusty baguette.

....

Kitchen Notes: If you have a Sunday with a bit of time, I suggest whipping up a double batch of Ann's Homemade Chicken Stock (page 41). If you just don't have the time, use either a fresh stock from your butcher or specialty food shop, or a box of good-quality low-sodium broth (I always have boxes of stock in my pantry).

Variation: This is also delicious with 2 handfuls of chopped fresh spinach added to the warm stock.

Elena's Curried Corn Chowder

Elena Embrioni, my vital recipe tester and contributor, makes wonderful soups—hearty and full of flavour. Like me, she doesn't typically write her recipes down. This corn chowder started with a soup of hers I love in her *Southern Accent* cookbook—a Cajun-style soup. After many variations, we added creamed corn and put tomatoes in at the end. The result is a cozy comfort meal in a bowl.

SERVES 6

INGREDIENTS

1 tbsp (15 mL) butter

1 tbsp (15 mL) olive oil

1 medium onion, chopped

1 tsp (5 mL) curry powder

8 baby new potatoes, quartered
 (or 2 medium Yukon Golds, peeled
 and cut into chunks)

Salt and pepper to taste

4 cups (1 L) fresh or thawed frozen
 corn kernels

1 sweet red pepper, diced

1/2 jalapeño or red chili pepper, finely diced

1/2 cup (125 mL) white wine

1 can (10 oz/284 mL) creamed corn

3 1/2 cups (875 mL) chicken stock

6 small tomatoes, coarsely chopped

1/2 cup (125 mL) 35% cream

Chives, for garnish

HOW TO

In a large heavy soup pot, melt butter with oil over medium-high heat. Add onion and sauté until soft, about 3 minutes. Add curry powder and sauté another minute. Stir in potatoes, salt and pepper; sauté another minute. Stir in corn kernels and cook until corn is lightly brown, about 5 minutes.

Stir in red pepper and jalapeño; sauté for another 2 minutes. Stir in wine and let evaporate. Add creamed corn and chicken stock, reduce heat to low and simmer 20 minutes.

Remove from heat. Remove two-thirds of the mixture and set aside. Using a hand blender, purée remaining soup in the pot. Return reserved soup to the pot.

Return to medium-high heat and add tomatoes and cream. Cook until heated through, about 5 minutes. Serve garnished with chives.

....

Variation: If you don't have a jalapeño or red chili, you can use 1 chipotle from the can, chopped—a great way to use up a pantry staple and add some smoky flavour.

Mulligatawny Soup

This is a family favourite—it's a meal in a bowl. One of my recipe testers, Stewie, adapted it from *Joy of Cooking*. It clears your sinuses if you have a cold, but the spices can be toned down by swirling 1 tbsp (15 mL) cream into each bowl just before serving. This is a great way to use up leftover chicken and rice.

SERVES 4

INGREDIENTS

2 tbsp (30 mL) olive oil

1/2 cup (125 mL) finely chopped onion

4 small carrots, finely chopped

2 stalks celery, finely chopped

1 to 2 tsp (5 to 10 mL) curry powder

4 tsp (20 mL) all-purpose flour

4 cups (1 L) chicken stock

1/2 cup (125 mL) cooked rice

1/2 cup (125 mL) diced cooked chicken

1/4 cup (60 mL) diced tart apples (such as Granny Smith)

1/4 tsp (1 mL) dried thyme

Salt and pepper to taste

1/2 cup (125 mL) 35% cream (optional)

HOW TO

In a large sauté pan, heat oil over medium heat. Sauté onion for 3 minutes or until slightly softened. Add carrots and celery and sauté a few more minutes, until they lightly change colour. Stir in curry powder. Stir in flour and cook, stirring constantly, for 3 minutes. Stir in chicken stock. Simmer for 30 minutes.

Add rice, chicken, apples and thyme. Simmer until heated through, 5 to 10 minutes. Season with salt and pepper.

Stir in cream, if using, just before serving.

....

Kitchen Notes: This doubles well and freezes well once completely cooled.

Curry powder: My favourite brand of curry is Bolts, which packs a punch, so you'd only need 1 tsp (5 mL) in this recipe. If you're using a mild curry powder, use 2 tsp (10 mL).

Bibby's Taco Soup

This is a down-home pantry essentials comfort soup. Check your fancy ideals at the door and get out the can opener! Our kids love "chili dippers"—chili with baked pitas or tortilla chips for dipping. This is a simple, yummy alternative. **SERVES 6 TO 8**

INGREDIENTS

1 tbsp (15 mL) olive oil

1 cup (250 mL) finely chopped onion

1 clove garlic, minced

1 1/2 lb (750 g) lean ground sirloin

1 can (28 oz/796 mL) diced tomatoes
   with juice

1 can (14 oz/398 mL) tomato sauce

1 can (14 oz/398 mL) black beans, drained
   and rinsed

1 can (about 1 cup/250 mL) corn kernels
   with juice

1 pkg (35 g) taco seasoning mix

Sour cream and grated Cheddar cheese,
   for garnish

HOW TO

In a large soup pot or sauté pan, heat oil over medium-high heat. Sauté onions for 5 minutes or until translucent. Add garlic and sauté for 1 more minute. Add beef and cook, stirring frequently and breaking it up with a wooden spoon, until browned, about 5 minutes. Add tomatoes, tomato sauce, beans, corn and taco seasoning. Reduce heat and simmer, uncovered, for 30 minutes. If it gets too thick, add a splash of stock or water.

Serve topped with sour cream and grated cheese, with a bowl of pita chips or nacho chips.

Grannie Annie's Magic Soup

This recipe is from a Georgian Bay cottage neighbour who loves to spend summer afternoons cooking up a storm. This family soup is said to magically chase away the sickies. I hope Ann doesn't mind that I gave the store-bought stock option for all of us time-pressed cooks who still want homemade soup . . . with a shortcut or two.   **SERVES 6**

INGREDIENTS

1 tbsp (15 mL) butter

2 tbsp (30 mL) olive oil

1 yellow onion, chopped

2 stalks celery, chopped

1 large carrot, chopped

1 leek (white part only), chopped

1 boiling potato, cut into small cubes

1 tsp (5 mL) dried marjoram

2 tbsp (30 mL) dry vermouth or white wine

6 cups (1.5 L) low-sodium chicken stock

1 tbsp (15 mL) cider vinegar

Kosher salt and pepper to taste

Chopped chives, for garnish

HOW TO

In a large saucepan, melt butter with olive oil over medium heat. Add onion and cook a few minutes, stirring occasionally. Stir in celery, carrot, leek and potato; cook a few more minutes. Stir in marjoram.

Turn heat up to high and carefully add vermouth, stirring to deglaze the pan until liquid has almost evaporated. Add stock, vinegar and salt and pepper. Bring to a boil, reduce heat and simmer until vegetables are tender, about 25 minutes. Taste, and adjust seasoning.

Remove from heat. Using a hand blender, carefully purée until smooth. Serve garnished with chives.

....

Variation: You can add a can of navy beans to make a heartier soup.

Homemade Chicken Stock

I know a few great home cooks who still make stock. It's why their soups are so flavourful. All it takes is a bit of organization to add some ingredients to your shopping list, and a lazy Sunday afternoon at home. **MAKES 6 TO 8 CUPS (1.5 TO 2 L)**

INGREDIENTS

Chicken carcass saved from a roast, or 3 chicken backs or 4 bone-in chicken breasts

1 yellow onion, chopped

2 stalks celery with leaves on, chopped

1 carrot, chopped

1 clove garlic, halved

1 slice fresh ginger

Bouquet garni (parsley stems, 12 peppercorns, 1 tsp/5 mL dried thyme, 1 tsp/5 mL dried sage, 1 large bay leaf, 1 clove and fresh herbs when you have them, tied in cheesecloth)

1 1/2 tsp (7 mL) salt, or to taste

HOW TO

In a large soup pot, put the chicken carcass, onion, celery, carrot, garlic, ginger and bouquet garni. Add enough cold water to just submerge chicken and vegetables.

Bring to a boil, then turn heat down to a simmer. Simmer at least an hour. Don't stir (it'll make the stock cloudy), but do skim off any scum that appears at the surface.

Strain stock through cheesecloth or a fine sieve, discarding solids. Season to taste. Cool completely. Store in an airtight container in the fridge for a week or freeze for up to 3 months.

Salads

Simple Greens with Keith's Tarragon Vinaigrette

Spring Greens with Creamy Vinaigrette

Arugula and Parm Salad with Lemon Vinaigrette

Skinnier Caesar Salad

Dutch Lettuce

Warm Spinach Salad

365 Days of 4 Wheel Farm Veggies

Summer Caprese Salad

Greek Vegetable Salad

Elena's Succotash

Picnic Chicken Salad

London Mango Salad

Wild Rice Salad

Bo's Coleslaw

Simple Greens with Keith's Tarragon Vinaigrette

An old friend's dad, Keith, always made the best simple salad. The trick is to have a good glass of wine in hand, enjoy the process and use good-quality ingredients.

SERVES 4

INGREDIENTS

4 large handfuls mixed baby or delicate greens (such as Bibb and red leaf)

VINAIGRETTE

2 tbsp (30 mL) red wine or balsamic vinegar

2 tsp (10 mL) plain yogurt

1 tsp (5 mL) Dijon mustard

1/2 tsp (2 mL) herbes de Provence

1/4 cup (60 mL) olive oil

2 tsp (5 mL) chopped fresh tarragon

Salt and pepper to taste

HOW TO

In a small bowl or measuring cup, whisk together vinegar, yogurt, mustard and herbes de Provence. Whisking constantly, slowly drizzle in olive oil; whisk until emulsified. Whisk in tarragon and season with salt and pepper.

Just before serving, put some of the vinaigrette in a salad bowl. Add lettuce and gently toss to coat, adding more dressing if needed. Season and serve.

....

Kitchen Notes: If you can find an old clay pot of herbes de Provence, leave it within reach on the counter for vinaigrettes, roasted vegetables and roast chicken.

Variations: Keith used sour cream, but yogurt is my preferred lighter way.
You can substitute tarragon vinegar for red wine or balsamic. Lighten the flavour by using half grapeseed oil and half olive oil.
Make an assertive dressing for hardier greens such as frisée by combining 1/2 cup (125mL) balsamic vinegar with 1 tbsp (15mL) Dijon mustard, 2 tbsp (30mL) maple syrup, 1 minced clove of garlic, 1/2 cup (125 mL) olive oil and salt and pepper to taste. Great with fruit, nut and cheese salads.

Spring Greens with Creamy Vinaigrette

If you time it right you may be able to find flowering pea shoots. They make a beautiful addition to this perfect springtime salad.

SERVES 6

INGREDIENTS

1/3 cup (75 mL) baby peas

1 bunch thin asparagus (about 12 stalks), ends snapped off

1 head red leaf lettuce

1 small head frisée or chicory

1/4 cup (60 mL) shaved pecorino cheese

VINAIGRETTE

3 tbsp (50 mL) sour cream

2 tbsp (30 mL) red wine vinegar

Salt and pepper

1/4 cup (60 mL) olive oil

HOW TO

Blanch peas in a pot of boiling salted water for 30 to 60 seconds. Transfer with a slotted spoon (don't drain the water) to a bowl of ice and cold water to stop the cooking. Drain well.

In the same pot, blanch asparagus until tender-crisp. Drain and plunge into a bowl of ice and cold water, then drain and pat dry. Cut on the diagonal into 1/2-inch (1 cm) pieces.

Wash, spin dry and tear the lettuces. Set aside.

To make the vinaigrette, in a small bowl whisk together sour cream, vinegar and salt and pepper. Slowly whisk in olive oil until emulsified.

Drizzle some of the dressing into a salad bowl. Add the lettuces and toss to lightly coat, adding more dressing if needed. Season with salt and pepper. (Reserve remaining dressing for a different salad the next night.) Top with asparagus, peas and pecorino.

Arugula and Parm Salad with Lemon Vinaigrette

A version of this salad appears on almost every Italian restaurant menu, and I order it almost every time. It's so easy to make at home—it's all about the best quality ingredients. Have lemons and a chunk of good Parmesan on hand at all times and you can entertain on short notice.

SERVES 4

INGREDIENTS

2 good handfuls baby arugula, washed and trimmed
1/4-lb (125 g) chunk Parmigiano-Reggiano

VINAIGRETTE

Zest of 1 lemon
2 tbsp (30 mL) fresh lemon juice (1 lemon)
1 tsp (5 mL) sugar
Salt and pepper to taste
1/4 cup (60 mL) good-quality olive oil

HOW TO

To make the vinaigrette, in a small bowl, combine lemon zest, lemon juice, sugar and salt and pepper. Whisking constantly, slowly drizzle in olive oil until emulsified. Taste, and adjust seasoning.

Drizzle some of the vinaigrette into a salad bowl. Add arugula and toss. Add more vinaigrette if needed. Season with salt and pepper.

Using a vegetable peeler, pull long curls off Parmesan. Garnish salad with curls of cheese.

....

Variation: Substitute balsamic vinegar for the lemon juice if you prefer. Intensify the balsamic flavour by heating the vinegar until slightly thickened.

IN MY MOTHER'S KITCHEN

Skinnier Caesar Salad

My sister-in law Nancy makes a great kid-friendly cheater version of Caesar salad at the cottage. Her secret is a store-bought dressing (she likes Renée's Caesar Dressing) thinned out and dressed up with fresh lemon juice and freshly grated Parmesan. Here is my version of this classic that's lower in fat but still full of Caesar flavour. **SERVES 4**

INGREDIENTS

1 large head romaine lettuce, outer leaves discarded
1/4 cup (60 mL) freshly grated or shaved Parmesan cheese
Parmesan curls
Cracked black pepper

DRESSING

2 cloves garlic, minced

1 tbsp (15 mL) fresh lemon juice

1 tsp (5 mL) horseradish

1/2 tsp (2 mL) Dijon mustard

1/4 tsp (1 mL) Worcestershire sauce

1/4 cup (60 mL) low-fat mayonnaise

2 tbsp (30 mL) plain yogurt

1/4 cup (60 mL) grated Parmesan cheese

Salt and freshly ground black pepper
   to taste

HOW TO

To make the dressing, in a small bowl whisk together garlic, lemon juice, horseradish, mustard and Worcestershire sauce. Whisk in mayonnaise, yogurt and grated Parmesan until a creamy consistency. Season with salt and pepper.

Tear lettuce into large pieces and place in a salad bowl. Add dressing and grated or shaved Parmesan and toss well. Top with Parmesan curls and cracked black pepper.

Serve with garlic bread: Cut a demi-baguette in half lengthwise. Mix 2 tbsp (30 mL) room-temperature butter with 1/2 tsp (2 mL) garlic powder and 1/2 tsp (2 mL) finely chopped parsley. Spread on bread. Wrap in foil and bake in a 400°F (200°C) oven for 15 to 20 minutes.

Variation: My friend Pauline's husband, Ron Ferguson, loves to cook. His Caesar has red onion, grilled portobellos, grilled pancetta and homemade croutons—a perfect salad as a main. Grill the portobellos, then slice. Toss the lettuce in the dressing, then top with red onion slices, portobello slices, pancetta and croutons for a jumbo composed salad.

Dutch Lettuce

This recipe is from my great-great-great-grandmother in Minnesota in the 1800s. Through letters we learned she was a great cook. One note read, "You must eat at the Lorette house." (That was her B & B.) Good cooks in our family go pretty far back. Sometimes this salad is referred to as "wilted lettuce." We love it with Friday-night burgers.

SERVES 2

INGREDIENTS

6 slices bacon
1 head leaf lettuce (about 12 large leaves)
2 1/2 tbsp (37 mL) white vinegar
2 tbsp (30 mL) 35% cream
1/2 tsp (2 mL) sugar
Pinch salt

HOW TO

Cook bacon until crisp. Drain on paper towels, reserving drippings in pan.

Meanwhile, wash and dry lettuce. Tear into large bite-size pieces and place in a salad bowl.

Pour hot bacon drippings over lettuce to lightly coat. Add vinegar, cream, sugar and salt. Crumble bacon in. Toss well and serve immediately.

....

Variation: You can also make the vinaigrette in the pan—add the vinegar, cream, sugar and salt to the hot bacon fat, give it a good stir, then pour over the lettuce.

Warm Spinach Salad

Louise Wright was the headmaster's wife at Trintiy College School, where my brothers all went for high school. She ran a gourmet cooking club for the boys, and some of her recipes are still my favourites a few decades later.

SERVES 6

INGREDIENTS

10 oz (300 g) fresh spinach (5 cups/1.25 L), washed, spun dry, tough stems removed
1/2 lb (250 g) bacon, strips cut into quarters
1/2 lb (250 g) cremini mushrooms, sliced
1 tbsp (15 mL) Dijon mustard
2 to 4 tbsp (30 to 60 mL) balsamic vinegar
Salt and pepper to taste

HOW TO

Put spinach in a large bowl.

In a cast-iron or other heavy frying pan, cook bacon over medium heat until crispy. Drain on paper towels.

Remove some of the bacon fat, leaving about 2 tbsp (30 mL). Add mushrooms and cook over medium heat until soft and brown, 3 to 4 minutes. Remove mushrooms and set aside.

Add mustard to the pan, stirring constantly with a wooden spoon. Add vinegar and stir constantly for 1 to 2 minutes or until combined and slightly thickened.

Pour hot vinaigrette over spinach, toss gently and season with salt and pepper. Top with mushrooms and bacon. Serve immediately.

365 Days of 4 Wheel Farm Veggies

My parents spend more than half their time at their 4 Wheel Farm (so named because you need the four-wheel drive to get up the road in the winter). My dad lives in his ever-growing garden and vineyard there.

FALL

Cauliflower—roasted or blanched

Broccoli—blanched

Peppers—grilled or roasted

Sweet potatoes—baked or mashed

Parsnips—baked fries

Endive—grilled

Radicchio—grilled

Fennel—braised

Onions—grilled

Squash—roasted

SPRING AND SUMMER

Asparagus—blanched, roasted or grilled

Leeks—grilled or roasted

Peas—blanched

Sugar snap peas—raw or blanched

Radishes—raw with salt or roasted

Carrots—raw or roasted

Green beans—blanched

Peppers—raw or grilled

Zucchini—raw or ribboned and sautéed

Cucumbers—raw, pickled

Endive—raw or grilled

Radicchio—raw or grilled

Celery—raw or braised

Eggplant—grilled

Tomatoes—raw or with oil and vinegar

To blanch vegetables, bring a large pot of salted water to a boil. Add vegetables and cook 10 to 20 seconds. Drain immediately and plunge into a bowl of cold water and ice to stop the cooking and maintain the vegetables' colour. Pat dry.

Summer Caprese Salad

This is a fun way to dress up summer tomatoes. When we were last in New York, fresh burrata cheese with tomatoes was on every menu. If you can find the coveted burrata, grab it for its deep flavour and great texture.

SERVES 4 TO 6

INGREDIENTS

8 oz (250 g) fresh mozzarella, sliced 1/2 inch (1 cm) thick
1 lb (500 g) field tomatoes, sliced 1/2 inch (1 cm) thick
Leaves from 2 large bunches basil

VINAIGRETTE

1 cup (250 mL) balsamic vinegar
1 tbsp (15 mL) Dijon mustard
1 clove garlic, minced
1/2 tsp (2 mL) salt
1/4 tsp (1 mL) freshly ground pepper
1/3 cup (75 mL) extra virgin olive oil

HOW TO

To make the vinaigrette, in a small saucepan, bring balsamic vinegar to a boil over medium heat. Reduce heat and simmer for 10 to 15 minutes or until reduced to 1/2 cup (125 mL). Let cool. It will thicken as it cools.

In a bowl, whisk together reduced vinegar, mustard, garlic, salt and pepper. Slowly drizzle in oil, whisking until emulsified.

Arrange cheese, tomatoes and basil leaves on a platter. Up to 1 hour before serving, drizzle with vinaigrette.

....

Variations: Make this into a pretty party hors d'oeuvre: wrap bite-size bocconcini in basil leaves and skewer with grape tomatoes. Drizzle with the vinaigrette and serve as finger food or arrange on a bed of greens.

Another fun option is to use sliced broiled feta in place of the mozzarella. Cut a large piece of feta into slices 1/2 inch (1 cm) thick, drizzle with olive oil and broil until golden. Serve on top of sliced field tomatoes and basil leaves drizzled with the vinaigrette.

Greek Vegetable Salad

This salad is a great complement to Greek-Style Chicken on a Stick (page 102). Perfect for a casual summer get-together.

SERVES 4

INGREDIENTS

2 medium tomatoes, chopped

1 large sweet red pepper, chopped

1/2 English cucumber, chopped

1/2 red onion, chopped

6 oz (175 g) feta, crumbled

Kalamata olives (optional)

VINAIGRETTE

2 tbsp (30 mL) fresh lemon juice

1 tsp (5 mL) chopped fresh oregano (or 1/2 tsp/2 mL dried)

1/4 cup (60 mL) good-quality olive oil

Salt and pepper to taste

HOW TO

In a salad bowl, combine chopped vegetables.

To make the vinaigrette, in a small bowl combine lemon juice and oregano. Slowly whisk in olive oil until emulsified. Season with salt and pepper.

One to 6 hours before serving, whisk vinaigrette again and toss with vegetables. Just before serving, gently toss in feta and olives, if using.

....

Kitchen Notes: This salad keeps well overnight, so leftovers for lunch the next day are just as yummy.

Greek staples: lemons, yogurt, garlic, oregano, feta, olives, onions.

Variation: Greek-style grilled veg salad from Ron: Grill 6 leeks, 6 portobello mushrooms, 2 sweet red peppers, 2 sweet yellow peppers and 2 sliced red onions. Toss in a bowl and top with kalamata olives and 8 oz (250 g) crumbled feta. Whisk together balsamic vinegar, whole grain mustard and olive oil and drizzle on top.

Elena's Succotash

This refreshing summer dish can be a salad, a side or a meal. Make it the day ahead—it's best the second day.

SERVES 6 TO 8

INGREDIENTS

Zest and juice of 1 lime

2 tsp (10 mL) butter, melted

1 tsp (5 mL) cayenne pepper

4 ears corn, husked

1 sweet red pepper, diced

1/4 red onion, diced

1 1/2 green onions, thinly sliced

1 1/2 cups (375 mL) halved cherry tomatoes

1 cup (250 mL) shelled edamame, blanched and cooled

1/3 cup (75 mL) olive oil

1 tsp (5 mL) salt

1 avocado, cubed (optional)

HOW TO

Preheat grill to medium.

Stir together lime zest, butter and cayenne. Brush on corn. Grill, turning every 3 or 4 minutes, until soft and lightly charred, about 10 minutes. Remove from grill and let cool.

Working over a large bowl, cut corn off the cob. Add red pepper, red onion, green onions, tomatoes, edamame, olive oil, salt and lime juice. Stir well. Cover and refrigerate overnight. Add avocado, if using, just before serving.

....

Kitchen Notes: I always buy edamame still in their shell for a quick snack, but for this dish, buy the shelled edamame to save time.

Variation: Substitute frozen fava beans for edamame.

Picnic Chicken Salad

This salad harkens back to my early catering days with my old friend Foofie. At twenty-one we were catering weddings on Georgian Bay island rocks and in fields in the rain. This was always a summer lunch entertaining favourite—make-ahead, delicious and all-in-one easy to serve.

SERVES 8

INGREDIENTS

1 large round loaf of bread (such as a boule or Calabrese loaf)

1/3 cup (75 mL) mayonnaise

1/2 tsp (2 mL) curry powder

1/4 tsp (1 mL) paprika

3 cups (750 mL) cubed cooked chicken (about 3 breasts)

1 cup (250 mL) green grapes, halved

1/2 cup (125 mL) chopped celery

1/2 cup (125 mL) sliced almonds, toasted

1/4 cup (60 mL) thinly sliced green onions

1 sweet red pepper, diced

Salt and black pepper

Romaine lettuce

HOW TO

Slice off the top 2 inches (5 cm) of the loaf in one big piece and set aside. Hollow out the bread, leaving a shell 1/2 inch (1 cm) thick.

In a medium bowl, stir together mayonnaise, curry powder and paprika. Stir in chicken, grapes, celery, almonds, green onion, red pepper, and salt and black pepper to taste.

Line the bread bowl with lettuce leaves. Spoon chicken mixture into the bread. Replace the bread top. Wrap tightly in plastic wrap and refrigerate until picnic time. (You can make the chicken salad the day before, and you can fill the bread half a day in advance.)

To serve, using a bread knife, slice the boule into wedges, so guests have ready-made sandwiches.

....

Kitchen Notes: In a pinch, buy a ready-to-go roasted chicken. Otherwise, roast boneless chicken breasts with a bit of salt and pepper, or do them my grandmother Bo's way, the most tender and flavourful: in a large pot of water, gently simmer chicken breasts with chopped onion, chopped celery, celery leaves, peppercorns, a bay leaf and parsley until cooked through, 20 to 30 minutes.

1 bone-in chicken breast yields about 1 cup (250 mL) cubed chicken.

1 large boneless chicken breast yields a generous cup (250 mL) cubed chicken.

To toast almonds, heat a dry frying pan over medium heat and dry-toast the nuts for a few minutes until light brown, stirring frequently.

Variation: This chicken salad is also delicious served on a bed of lettuce or on grilled flatbread or crostini.

London Mango Salad

Tori brought this recipe back from her life in London. I love to serve this salad with grilled chicken or fish.

SERVES 4 TO 6

INGREDIENTS

3 ripe mangoes (Alphonso), peeled and thinly sliced
1 sweet red pepper, thinly sliced
1/4 red onion, thinly sliced
1/2 cup (125 mL) chiffonade of fresh basil
1/2 cup (125 mL) finely chopped fresh mint

VINAIGRETTE

Zest of 1 lime
1/4 cup (60 mL) fresh lime juice (2 limes)
2 tsp (10 mL) sugar
1/2 tsp (2 mL) hot pepper flakes
1/4 tsp (1 mL) salt
1 tbsp (15 mL) grapeseed oil
Black pepper

HOW TO

To make the vinaigrette, combine lime zest, lime juice, sugar, hot pepper flakes and salt. Slowly drizzle in oil and whisk until emulsified. Season with black pepper.

Combine mangoes, red pepper and onion in a salad bowl.

One to 3 hours before serving, whisk dressing again and gently toss with salad. Add basil and mint up to 30 minutes before serving.

....

Kitchen Notes: This is still delicious the next day.

I love the Alphonso mangoes—they are yellow, small and super sweet.

To speed up ripening, put mangoes in a paper bag at room temperature. Ripe mangoes will keep in the fridge for a few days.

To chiffonade, roll herb leaves tightly and slice thinly on an angle.

When chopping delicate herbs like mint and basil, chop only once so you don't bruise them.

Variation: To make this even simpler, replace the vinaigrette with lime juice to taste.

Wild Rice Salad

My old university roommate Lynn used to make this for our house of eight. It was great for dinner and lunch again the next day. One of our favourite restaurants in Kingston, Chez Piggy, always had great rice, legume and veggie dishes. This salad is a mix of ideas from Lynnie's mom and from Chez Piggy.

SERVES 6 TO 8

INGREDIENTS

2 cups (500 mL) mixed rice (wild and long-grain), cooked, rinsed and cooled

1/2 cup (125 mL) bean sprouts

1/2 cup (125 mL) golden raisins or currants

1/2 cup (125 mL) chopped snow peas

1/2 cup (125 mL) chopped parsley

1/4 cup (60 mL) finely chopped green onions

4 stalks celery, finely chopped

1 sweet red pepper, finely chopped

VINAIGRETTE

3 tbsp (50 mL) sesame seeds

1 tbsp (15 mL) honey

1 clove garlic, minced

1/4 cup (60 mL) fresh orange juice

1 tbsp (15 mL) cider vinegar

1 tbsp (15 mL) tamari

1/4 cup (60 mL) vegetable oil

1 tbsp (15 mL) sesame oil

HOW TO

In a large bowl, combine all salad ingredients.

In a small bowl, combine sesame seeds, honey and garlic. Whisk in orange juice, vinegar and tamari. Slowly whisk in vegetable oil and sesame oil, whisking constantly until emulsified.

Pour vinaigrette over rice salad and stir to combine. Refrigerate at least 3 hours before serving.

Bo's Coleslaw

This is a sweet-and-sour vinaigrette coleslaw, not a creamy one, so it's perfect for summer picnics and certainly lower cal. This coleslaw is a Friday-night classic of my mom's at the farm, served with burgers (page 132).   **SERVES 8 TO 10**

INGREDIENTS

1 medium green cabbage, cored and finely shredded

2 carrots, finely shredded

2 green onions, finely chopped

1/4 cup (60 mL) sugar

VINAIGRETTE

1/2 cup (125 mL) sugar

1/3 cup (75 mL) white vinegar

1 tbsp (15 mL) prepared mustard

1 tsp (5 mL) salt

1 tsp (5 mL) celery seeds

1/3 cup (75 mL) vegetable oil

HOW TO

In a large bowl, toss shredded vegetables with sugar.

In a medium pot, combine sugar, vinegar, mustard, salt and celery seeds; bring to a boil. Carefully add oil. Boil 1 more minute. Pour over vegetables. Mix with a fork. Cover tightly and marinate, refrigerated, at least 5 hours. Coleslaw keeps, refrigerated, up to 3 days.

....

Kitchen Notes: Celery seed is a must for this dish.

To shred vegetables finely, use a food processor with the slicing disc or do it by hand with a sharp knife. Shred carrots with a box grater.

Variations: My mom always uses green cabbage, but I love the deep purple too (we use it along with julienned mango in Greg Couillard's slaw found in my book dish entertains).

For a version with napa cabbage, add toasted sesame seeds and ramen noodles.

Mains
[pasta, etc.]

Mac and Cheese

The Pasta Lowdown

Pasta Quickie with Tomatoes, Olives and Basil

Spaghettini with Sun-Dried Tomatoes, Roasted Red Peppers and Spinach

Hamptons Girls' Weekend Tuscan Pasta

Spag Bol

Bowties alla Carbonara

Cheese Soufflé

Risotto

Ham, Cheese and Spinach Strata

Mac and Cheese

We tested this recipe more than any other in this book, or so it feels. The goal was the perfect mac and cheese for kids as well as adults. My sister-in-law Amanda's mom, Wendy, gave us her recipe, and we loved her tangy mayo addition, and I took direction from our kids, whose favourite (until now!) was a prepared mac and cheese with big chunky croutons with paprika. This recipe has just a touch of spice, but feel free to add a bit more cayenne. The penne noodle won, and the key is tons of sauce.

SERVES 8 TO 10

INGREDIENTS

3 tbsp (50 mL) butter

3 tbsp (50 mL) all-purpose flour

1 1/2 tsp (7 mL) salt

1/4 tsp (1 mL) black pepper

2 1/2 cups (625 mL) milk

1/2 tsp (2 mL) dry mustard

1/4 tsp (1 mL) cayenne pepper

1 1/2 cups (375 mL) grated extra-old
   Cheddar cheese

1/4 cup (60 mL) mayonnaise

3 cups (750 mL) penne

1/2 cup (125 mL) coarsely chopped ham

TOPPING

1/2 cup (125 mL) large chunky dry bread
   crumbs

1/2 cup (125 mL) grated Parmigiano-
   Reggiano

1/2 tsp (2 mL) paprika

2 tbsp (30 mL) butter, melted

HOW TO

Preheat oven to 375°F (190°C).

In a medium saucepan, melt butter over medium heat. Stir in flour, salt and black pepper; cook, stirring constantly, for 2 minutes. Gradually add milk, whisking constantly. Add dry mustard and cayenne. Cook, stirring often, until thickened. Remove from heat and stir in cheese and mayonnaise.

Cook pasta in boiling salted water until al dente. Drain pasta and put back into pot. Stir in cheese sauce and ham. Turn mixture into a 9- x 13-inch (3 L) casserole dish.

To make the topping, in a small bowl, stir together bread crumbs, Parmesan and paprika. Stir in melted butter. Spread topping over macaroni.

Bake for 20 minutes or until bubbling. Turn oven to broil and broil for 3 minutes or until top is golden brown.

Serve with salsa, Lee and Bo's Tomato Butter (page 186) or chili sauce.

....

Variation: Feel free to veg this up with a cup or so of peas, broccoli, roasted cherry tomatoes or more ham. If adding peas or broccoli, add them to the pasta pot a minute or so before the pasta is done to blanch them.

The Pasta Lowdown

I find it tough to commit pasta dishes to paper. I make pasta at least once a week and never the same way twice. It often has a sort of progression to it, one dish for the kids, then add-ins for the parents. Below are all kinds of choices to keep your pastas interesting. Just follow the basic steps and you'll soon be freestyling pasta like a pro.

Fill a large pasta pot with cold water and bring it to a rolling boil on high heat. Add salt.

Get out your favourite sauté pan (mine is a 6-quart/6 L All-Clad with straight sides) and tongs or a wooden spoon.

Pick your pasta—penne, farfalle, spaghetti, ravioli, etc.

Pick your oil—olive oil, while best for flavour, is meant to be consumed raw or cooked only at low temps. For cooking, use veg, sunflower, safflower, grapeseed or canola oil—one with a high smoke point that lets you sauté without burning. Put some oil in your pan and heat it over medium-high heat.

Start with onions—sweet Vidalia, shallots, red, green, plain ol' white—you choose. With the exception of green onions, they go first into the pan with the oil. Sauté a few minutes, until translucent.

Meats (optional)—bacon, pancetta, prosciutto, ham—finely chop and sauté with the onion.

Dried vegetables to rehydrate—mushrooms, sun-dried tomatoes—first place in a bowl and cover with boiling water to rehydrate, then drain.

Vegetables to blanch—broccoli and cauliflower are best with a quick blanch to help soften them and maintain their colour.

Vegetables to quickly sauté—roasted red peppers from a jar, fresh mushrooms, tomatoes—cut them up bite-size and sauté in the same sauté pan a few minutes.

Wine to deglaze.

Sauce—tomato sauce (store-bought or tomatoes from a can or your homemade) goes in now, or cream brought to a boil and reduced, or both or neither.

Fresh herbs, chopped, and/or garlic get added here.

Drain the pasta, reserving some pasta water to help with desired consistency, and add the pasta to the sauté pan.

Fresh greens—baby arugula or spinach—get added now, then turn the heat off.

Add reserved pasta water if necessary for desired consistency.

Cheese—add it now—feta, Parm, chèvre, Gorgonzola, whatever cheese you love and have.

Plate—use big pasta bowls and tongs. Twirl long pasta as you put it into the bowl to create a mound.

Season—finish with cracked pepper and grated cheese.

Enjoy!

Pasta Quickie with Tomatoes, Olives and Basil

This easy pasta follows my "Pasta Lowdown" principles and is a great empty fridge supper.

SERVES 4

INGREDIENTS

2 tbsp (30 mL) olive oil

1 small onion, finely chopped

2 cans (each 28 oz/796 mL) good-quality Italian plum tomatoes

1 tsp (5 mL) sugar

3 tbsp (50 mL) balsamic vinegar

1 lb (500 g) penne

1/2 cup (125 mL) pitted kalamata olives, halved

Salt and pepper to taste

Leaves from 1 bunch basil, coarsely chopped

3/4 cup (175 mL) grated pecorino cheese

HOW TO

In a medium sauté pan, heat oil over medium heat. Add onion and cook, stirring frequently, for 4 minutes or until softened. Add tomatoes with their juice. Add sugar. Reduce heat and simmer for 1 minute, squishing tomatoes with the back of a wooden spoon. Stir in vinegar and remove from heat.

Cook pasta in a large pot of boiling salted water until al dente. Drain pasta, reserving 1/2 cup (125 mL) pasta water, and return pasta to the pot.

Off the heat, toss pasta with tomato sauce. Add olives and enough pasta water to give desired consistency. Season with salt and pepper. Quickly toss in basil and 1/2 cup (125 mL) pecorino and serve immediately. Pass remaining pecorino at the table.

....

Kitchen Notes: In the summertime, use 2 lb (1 kg) fresh local tomatoes—grape, cherry or small vine-ripened—cut in half, tossed with oil, vinegar, salt and pepper, then tossed with cooked hot pasta. You may need to add a bit more oil.

Variations: A welcome addition is 1/2 cup (125 mL) cooked chopped spicy Italian sausage. Substitute crumbled feta for the pecorino.

Spaghettini with Sun-Dried Tomatoes, Roasted Red Peppers and Spinach

This casual around-the-counter dinner is bursting with flavour and justifiably worth the few drops of cream. An ideal pantry pasta, it uses simple ingredients on hand. Add rehydrated dried or fresh mushrooms or olives—whatever inspires you from your pantry or fridge.

SERVES 4 TO 6

INGREDIENTS

2 tbsp (30 mL) butter

1 tbsp (15 mL) olive oil

2 shallots, minced (about 1/4 cup/60 mL)

1/2 cup (125 mL) sun-dried tomatoes, drained and chopped

1/2 cup (125 mL) drained jarred roasted red peppers, chopped

2/3 cup (150 mL) 35% cream

1/4 cup (60 mL) chiffonade of fresh basil

1 cup (250 mL) fresh baby spinach

Salt and black pepper to taste

1 lb (500 g) spaghettini

1/4 cup (60 mL) grated Parmesan cheese

HOW TO

Bring a large pot of salted water to a boil.

In a large sauté pan, melt butter with oil over medium-high heat. Add shallots and sauté for 1 minute. Add sun-dried tomatoes and sauté 1 more minute. Add roasted peppers and sauté 1 more minute. Add cream. Bring to a boil and cook, stirring, until sauce thickens, about 4 minutes. Reduce heat to low and stir in basil. Remove sauce from heat, stir in spinach and season with salt and pepper. Keep sauce warm.

Cook pasta until al dente. Drain, reserving about 1 cup (250 mL) pasta water. Toss pasta with sauce, adding a little pasta water if necessary for desired consistency. Serve immediately, topped with Parmesan.

....

Kitchen Notes: To chiffonade, roll herb leaves tightly and slice thinly at an angle.

Variations: Oven-roasted tomatoes can be a substitute or addition to this pasta (or your favourite pasta, pizza, risotto or salad): Slice plum, Roma or Campari tomatoes lengthwise, place on a baking sheet, drizzle with olive oil, sprinkle with salt and pepper, and roast at 450°F (230°C) for 20 minutes. Towards the end, drizzle with balsamic vinegar if serving on top of greens.
You can substitute almond milk for the cream.
Crumbled cooked bacon (1/4 lb/125 g) is a great addition.

Hamptons Girls' Weekend
Tuscan Pasta

Once a year our university house has a get-together. Recently Tori and I made a big pasta, and it was a hit with all eight women. It was fresh, simple and easy to do. **SERVES 4 TO 6**

INGREDIENTS

5 cups (1.25 L) cherry tomatoes, halved (or 1 lb/500 g large tomatoes, diced)

1/4 cup (60 mL) olive oil

Salt and black pepper to taste

1 clove garlic, minced

1/4 tsp (1 mL) hot pepper flakes

1 tbsp (15 mL) balsamic vinegar

1 lb (500 g) linguine

1 cup (250 mL) halved pitted kalamata olives

2 tbsp (30 mL) chopped fresh basil

2 handfuls baby arugula, coarse stems removed

6 oz (175 g) chèvre, crumbled

1/4 cup (60 mL) freshly grated Parmesan cheese

HOW TO

Preheat oven to 425°F (220°C).

Place tomatoes on a parchment-lined baking sheet, drizzle with 2 tbsp (30 mL) of the olive oil and season with salt and black pepper. Roast tomatoes 20 minutes or until soft and golden. Remove from oven. Sprinkle garlic, hot pepper flakes and balsamic vinegar over tomatoes and stir gently. Turn oven off and return baking sheet to oven to keep warm. Keep an eye on it, though—the balsamic can burn.

Cook noodles in boiling salted water until al dente. Drain, reserving 1 cup (250 mL) pasta water, and return pasta to the pot.

Off the heat, add olives, basil, arugula, tomatoes with their juices and remaining 2 tbsp (30 mL) oil. Using tongs, gently toss. Add chèvre and Parmesan; gently toss with tongs until incorporated. Add some of the reserved pasta water if necessary for desired consistency. Season with salt and pepper and serve immediately.

Spag Bol

While this dish doesn't have a traditional rich, thick Bolognese sauce, it is a hearty meat-and-veg pasta that feeds a crowd easily. My kids picked up the name from the Fowler household and it stuck. Serve with homemade garlic bread (page 51) and everyone will be happy.

SERVES 6 TO 8

INGREDIENTS

2 tbsp (30 mL) vegetable oil

1 cup (250 mL) finely chopped yellow onion
   (1 medium)

1/2 cup (125 mL) finely chopped celery

1 1/2 lb (750 g) lean ground beef

1/2 cup (125 mL) finely chopped mushrooms

1 tsp (5 mL) dried oregano

2 cloves garlic, minced

2 cans (each 28 oz/796 mL) puréed tomatoes

2 tbsp (30 mL) ketchup

1/4 cup (60 mL) chopped fresh basil

1 tbsp (15 mL) chopped parsley

1 tbsp (15 mL) balsamic vinegar

Kosher salt and pepper to taste

1 1/2 lb (750 g) spaghetti

Freshly grated Parmesan cheese

HOW TO

In a large heavy frying pan, heat oil over medium heat. Add onion and sauté until translucent, 3 to 5 minutes. Add celery and sauté 2 minutes more. Add ground beef and sauté, stirring frequently and breaking it up with a wooden spoon, until browned, about 10 minutes. Spoon off all but 2 tsp (10 mL) fat.

Add mushrooms and oregano and cook 2 to 3 minutes more. Add garlic and cook 1 more minute. Stir in tomatoes and ketchup, scraping up browned bits on bottom of pan. Reduce heat to low and simmer, uncovered and stirring occasionally, for 45 minutes or more, until thick.

Stir in basil, parsley and vinegar; season well with salt and pepper.

Cook spaghetti in boiling salted water until al dente. Serve sauce over spaghetti and pass the grated Parmesan.

....

Kitchen Notes: The secret to a good spaghetti sauce is a long, low simmer. This sauce tastes even better the next day.

Variations: Leftover sauce can be turned into tacos the next day. Simply add a 35 g package of taco seasoning and simmer. Warm taco shells and set grated cheese, lettuce, cucumbers and salsa out for a self-serve taco party. One dinner two ways!

Make a Simple Pantry Tomato Sauce: Brown 1/2 lb (250 g) ground beef; set aside in pan. Place in a blender 1 can (28 oz/796 mL) plum tomatoes with juice, 1 can (14 oz/398 mL) Italian tomato sauce, 1 can (10 oz/284 mL) tomato juice, 2 tbsp (30 mL) tomato paste, 3 tbsp (50 mL) sugar and 1 chopped medium onion. Purée. Add to meat, bring to a boil, season with salt and pepper, and simmer, uncovered, for several hours.

Bowties alla Carbonara

I found a variation of this recipe on a worn recipe card at my parents' cottage, from the previous owner, Mrs. Warrington. It's well over thirty years old, but it has become an "old is new again" family favourite. This is not for the faint of heart. The bacon and eggs make this dish taste like breakfast, comfort casual—and a great meal the night before a soccer game or cross-country meet. Serve with a simple green salad. **SERVES 4 TO 6**

INGREDIENTS

3 eggs

1/2 cup (125 mL) grated Parmesan cheese

1/3 cup plus 2 tbsp (100 mL) 35% cream

1/2 tsp (2 mL) salt

Cracked black pepper to taste

1/2 lb (250 g) bacon, cut into medium pieces

1/4 cup (60 mL) finely chopped onion

3 tbsp (50 mL) white wine

1 lb (500 g) farfalle

1/2 cup (125 mL) fresh or frozen peas

2 tsp (10 mL) chopped fresh sage or thyme

HOW TO

Bring a large pot of salted water to a boil.

Meanwhile, in a small bowl, beat eggs. Whisk in Parmesan, cream and salt and pepper; mix well. Set aside.

In a large frying pan, cook bacon until brown; transfer to paper towels to drain. Spoon off all but 1 tsp (5 mL) fat. Add onion and sauté until translucent. Carefully add wine, stirring to get bits off the bottom of the pan. Remove from heat and keep warm.

Cook pasta. Two minutes before pasta is al dente, add peas. Drain, reserving about 1 cup (250 mL) of the pasta water. Return pasta and peas to the pot.

Off the heat, toss warm onion-wine mixture with pasta. Immediately add egg mixture, tossing pasta with tongs to prevent eggs from overcooking and sticking to bottom of pot. Add some of the pasta water if needed for desired consistency. Add reserved bacon, season with sage and cracked pepper, and serve immediately.

Variation: Use penne or fettuccine instead of farfalle.

Cheese Soufflé

Soufflés are a throwback to the '70s when many a domestic goddess would show off her cooking prowess by serving a towering soufflé to guests. It's one of those dishes, like a cheese sauce or risotto, that with a little practice is a cinch. My mom makes a cheese soufflé mid-week for no occasion—she thinks it's that easy. (And it is, really!) Serve with Lee and Bo's Tomato Butter (page 186) or stewed tomatoes and sausages. Breakfast for dinner! **SERVES 3 OR 4**

INGREDIENTS

3 tbsp (50 mL) butter

3 tbsp (50 mL) all-purpose flour

1 cup (250 mL) milk

1/2 tsp (2 mL) dry mustard

Pinch cayenne pepper

1 cup (250 mL) grated aged Cheddar cheese

4 eggs, separated

Salt and black pepper to taste

HOW TO

Preheat oven to 325°F (160°C).

In a heavy saucepan, melt butter over medium heat. Add flour and cook, stirring constantly, 2 minutes. Slowly add milk, stirring constantly, and cook, stirring, until thick and smooth. Add dry mustard and cayenne. Stir in cheese until melted. Set aside to cool.

Beat egg yolks until thick and pale yellow. Season with salt and pepper. Stir into cooled cheese sauce.

In a large bowl, using a whisk or electric mixer, beat egg whites until stiff but not dry. Do not over-beat. Carefully but thoroughly fold egg whites into cheese sauce—do not over-mix and deflate the egg whites. Pour into an ungreased soufflé dish.

Bake until soufflé has risen and the top is light golden brown, 35 to 40 minutes. (Peek through the oven window at 30 minutes but don't open the door. Make sure your oven window is clean so you can see!) Serve immediately.

....

Kitchen Notes: Bring right to the table—it's so impressive! Have spectators ready to cheer because it falls quickly.

My mom prefers an ungreased dish so the batter "creeps and walks up the sides."

Variations: You can add caramelized onions (cook 1 finely chopped onion in the butter at the start), bacon (5 strips cooked and cut into small pieces) and/or 2 cups (500 mL) fresh baby spinach (folded in with the egg whites).

My mom prefers orange Cheddar to give a deep golden colour, but you can certainly use white.

Risotto

This basic risotto recipe has endless variations. Knowing the basics means you'll never be without a great supper idea. Mushroom risotto is a mid-week staple in our home—everyone loves it, and all I need is good-quality pantry ingredients and a little time to stand and stir. When the kids ask about the little brown pieces (mushrooms), I stretch the truth just a bit—"it's just part of what comes from the earth"—and they gobble the risotto up.

SERVES 3 OR 4

INGREDIENTS

5 to 6 cups (1.25 to 1.5 L) low-sodium chicken stock

2 tbsp (30 mL) olive oil

3 tbsp (50 mL) butter

1 medium sweet onion, finely chopped

1 cup (250 mL) finely chopped cremini mushrooms

1 1/2 cups (375 mL) Carnaroli, Vialone Nano or arborio rice

1/2 cup (125 mL) white wine

1 cup (250 mL) freshly grated Parmesan cheese

Kosher salt and freshly ground pepper

HOW TO

Heat stock in a saucepan and keep at a gentle simmer.

In a large sauté pan, heat olive oil and 2 tbsp (30 mL) of the butter over medium heat; add onion and cook, stirring often, for 5 minutes. Add mushrooms and cook for 2 to 3 minutes, until mushrooms are softened.

Stir in rice. Let rice fry a bit with the onions, stirring often. After a minute it will look slightly translucent. Add wine and keep stirring, letting liquid cook off.

Add 1/2 cup (125 mL) of hot stock. Turn down the heat to a brisk simmer so the rice doesn't cook too quickly on the outside. Stir until almost all the stock is absorbed but the rice is not dry, then add another 1/2 cup (125 mL) of stock, stirring constantly. Carry on adding stock until rice is soft but still has a slight bite and there's still a bit of liquid in the pan. This will take 17 to 20 minutes. Turn off the heat.

Quickly stir in the remaining 1 tbsp (15 mL) butter and the Parmesan. Season well with salt and pepper. Stir gently. Serve immediately so the risotto retains its creamy texture.

Kitchen Notes: The ratio of rice to liquid is about 1:4. A generous main for 2 requires 1 cup (250 mL) of uncooked rice and about 4 cups (1 L) stock.

Cook your risotto in a shallow layer so it will cook evenly. A sauté pan or frying pan is better than a saucepan or stock pot. My favourite pan for risotto is a heavy 6-quart (6 L) sauté pan.

Variations: Substitute seasonal veg throughout the year—spring (asparagus, leeks, peas), summer (tomatoes), fall (mushrooms, beets).

Lobster and Tomato Risotto: Chop up the meat from thawed frozen lobster claws and add halfway through with diced tomatoes. This is a delicious combination.

Pesto and Pea Risotto: Add frozen baby peas 3 minutes before risotto is done. Once cooking is complete, turn off heat, stir in 1 to 2 tbsp (15 to 30 mL) pesto, then swirl in the Parmesan.

Ham, Cheese and Spinach Strata

This is truly a dish that works for grown-ups and kids alike. My son, Fin, made a list of the ten dinners that he "approved," and this was No. 4 (the "wifesaver"!). My first version had just bacon and cheese, then I put spinach in and it still got both thumbs up. You can serve this for dinner with a salad, but I like it best as brunch for a multi-generational crowd. **SERVES 6 TO 8**

INGREDIENTS

3 tbsp (50 mL) butter

1 medium onion, finely chopped

3/4 lb (375 g) thinly sliced Black forest ham, cut in wide ribbons

6 cups (1.5 L) baby spinach, washed, dried and coarsely chopped

2 cups (500 mL) grated Gruyère

1 cup (250 mL) grated Parmigiano-Reggiano

1 baguette, cut into 1-inch (2.5 cm) cubes (about 7 cups/1.75 L)

9 large eggs

3 cups (750 mL) 2% milk

2 tbsp (30 mL) Dijon mustard

2 tsp (10 mL) dry mustard

1 tsp (5 mL) kosher salt

1/4 tsp (1 mL) nutmeg

A few pinches cayenne pepper

Black pepper to taste

HOW TO

Butter a deep 9- x 13-inch (3 L) gratin dish.

In a heavy frying pan, melt butter over medium heat. Add onion and cook, stirring occasionally, until soft, about 4 minutes. Add ham and cook lightly. Remove from heat and add spinach, using tongs to incorporate.

Mix cheeses together. Spread one-third of the bread in the gratin dish. Top with one-third of the spinach mixture. Sprinkle with one-third of the cheese. Repeat layering, ending with cheese on top.

In a large bowl, whisk together eggs, milk, Dijon, dry mustard, salt, nutmeg, cayenne and black pepper. Pour evenly over strata. Cover and refrigerate 6 to 8 hours. Bring to room temperature before baking.

Preheat oven to 350°F (180°C). Uncover strata and bake for 50 minutes or until bread is golden and eggs are set. Let stand a few minutes before serving.

....

Kitchen Notes: You can get this ready in the morning and bake it at night for dinner, or prepare it the day before, bake for 30 minutes, then reheat before serving.

In place of fresh spinach, you can use a 10-oz (284 g) package of frozen spinach, thawed and squeezed dry.

Mains
[fish & chicken]

Bonnie's Barbecued Salmon

Summer Poached Salmon

Stewie's Oven-Roasted Salmon

Spicy Caribbean Curried Shrimp

Simple Sole Meunière

Lake of the Woods Cheater Salt-and-Vinegar Chips Fish Fry

Greek-Style Chicken on a Stick with Grilled Pita

Thai Chicken on a Stick with Peanut Sauce

Korean Chicken Thighs

Chicken Drumettes

Mom's Zephyr Island Barbecued Pineapple Chicken

Chicken and Broccoli Casserole

Mock Butter Chicken

Chicken with Morels

Coq au Vin

Jamaican Shediac Cape Curry

No-Fail Roast Chicken

Thanksgiving or Christmas Turkey

Bonnie's Barbecued Salmon

This delicious salmon looks beautiful—impressive to serve guests at a casual gathering. For a large group, ask for a whole side of salmon. I prefer wild Atlantic salmon.   **SERVES 5 OR 6**

INGREDIENTS

1 centre-cut side of salmon (2 1/2 lb/1.25 kg), 2 inches (5 cm) thick

1 clove garlic, crushed

1 tbsp (15 mL) pepper

1 tbsp (15 mL) chopped parsley

1 tbsp (15 mL) maple syrup

1 tbsp (15 mL) soy sauce

1 tbsp (15 mL) vegetable oil

HOW TO

Preheat grill to medium-high.

Place salmon on a large sheet of foil. In a small bowl, combine garlic, pepper, parsley, maple syrup, soy sauce and oil. Brush sauce all over the fish. Tent top of foil.

Grill 12 to 15 minutes or until flesh is nearly opaque in the centre. Remove from heat. Spoon sauce over fish.

....

Variation: Instead of foil, you can grill the salmon on a soaked cedar plank. With the lid down, on medium heat, the salmon will take 25 to 30 minutes.

Summer Poached Salmon

In my early catering days, poached salmon was a popular request. I used to order a whole side already poached from my fishmonger, because I didn't have a pan large enough for a whole side! Later I learned that a roasting pan across two burners does the trick. Better yet, ask for centre-cut fillets—much easier on the cook.

SERVES 6

INGREDIENTS

1 carrot, chopped

1 onion, chopped

1 stalk celery, chopped

1 bay leaf

2 tbsp (30 mL) chopped parsley

1 tsp (5 mL) peppercorns

1 tsp (5 mL) salt

1 cup (250 mL) white wine

6 centre-cut salmon fillets, each 4 to 6 oz (125 to 175 g)

HOW TO

In a 6-quart (6 L) sauté pan or large frying pan with high sides, combine carrot, onion, celery, bay leaf, parsley, peppercorns, salt, wine and 6 to 8 cups (1.5 to 2 L) water. Bring to a boil, then reduce heat and simmer for 5 minutes to flavour the water.

Using a slotted spatula, carefully lower salmon fillets into simmering water. Gently poach the salmon for 5 to 8 minutes or until outsides have just set and lost their clear flesh colour (8 minutes per inch/2.5 cm of thickness). Do not overcook. Carefully lift fillets from the pan and transfer to a plate lined with paper towels to absorb excess water.

Serve immediately with a mango salsa or a garlicky lemon-dill mayo (see Kitchen Notes below).

....

Kitchen Notes: For a quick mango salsa, combine 1 diced peeled mango, 1/2 diced sweet red pepper, 1/4 cup (60 mL) chopped fresh basil and the zest and juice of 1 lime.

To make a quick and simple garlicky lemon-dill mayo, add chopped fresh dill, crushed garlic and fresh lemon juice to store-bought mayo.

Stewie's Oven-Roasted Salmon aka Fish in Disguise

I admit fish is not my favourite. It's not my mom's favourite either. But I love all three of the salmon recipes in this book. These are for all of you who need your fish in disguise. Stewie's barbecue sauce is actually from Frannie, an excellent Vancouver cook. This preparation is anything but gourmet and everything delicious.

SERVES 6

INGREDIENTS

6 centre-cut salmon fillets, each 5 oz (150 g)
1/2 cup (125 mL) butter
1/4 cup (60 mL) ketchup
2 tbsp (30 mL) soy sauce
1 tbsp (15 mL) prepared mustard
1 clove garlic, crushed

HOW TO

Preheat oven to 425°F (220°C). Line a baking sheet with parchment paper and place salmon on baking sheet.

In a small pot, combine butter, ketchup, soy sauce, mustard and garlic. Cook over medium heat, whisking frequently, until thickened. Brush salmon with half the sauce.

Bake for 8 to 10 minutes per inch (2.5 cm). Serve salmon with remaining sauce.

Spicy Caribbean Curried Shrimp

This is a great appetizer or light dinner. I made this one night for just Bryce and me, and to my surprise, our son, Fin, tried a shrimp off my plate and said, "That's good, Mom! What is it?" Shocking from our picky eater, and a testament to the fact that kids like flavour and even a bit of heat.

SERVES 4 TO 6

INGREDIENTS

2 tbsp (30 mL) grapeseed oil

2 shallots, finely chopped

2 green onions, finely chopped

3 cloves garlic, minced

1 tbsp (15 mL) curry powder

1 jalapeño pepper, seeded and minced

2 lb (1 kg) fresh shrimp, peeled and deveined

Salt and pepper to taste

2 tsp (10 mL) fresh lime juice

2 tbsp (30 mL) butter

HOW TO

In a heavy sauté pan or frying pan with high sides, heat oil over medium-high heat. Sauté shallots, green onions and garlic for 2 minutes or until fragrant and translucent. Add curry powder and cook, stirring, 2 minutes.

Add jalapeño and shrimp. Sprinkle with salt and pepper. Cook shrimp, turning occasionally, until they just turn pink, about 3 minutes. Do not overcook—shrimp should be firm but tender. Stir in lime juice and butter. Taste, and adjust seasoning.

Serve immediately over rice.

. . . .

Variations: If you want more substance, add 1/2 cup (125 mL) coconut milk and 1/4 cup (60 mL) chicken stock before the shrimp to create a sauce.

Serve the shrimp on skewers for a stand-up dinner.

Reduce the curry and jalapeño and the kids will eat the shrimp!

Marinate in the same ingredients (minus the butter) for 30 minutes, skewer, then grill about 1 minute per side.

Simple Sole Meunière

Pan-fried with lemon is how my dad used to cook his freshly caught Georgian Bay bass. Later I discovered this was an age-old classic French dish. The first time I made this for my kids, I was nervous they wouldn't go for it, since they were so used to baked fish sticks. But Fin fell in love with it, and it immediately went on his "Fin's Dinners" list. **SERVES 4**

INGREDIENTS

1/3 cup (75 mL) all-purpose flour

Kosher salt and freshly ground black pepper

4 sole fillets, each 5 oz (150 g)

2 tbsp (30 mL) grapeseed oil

2 tbsp (30 mL) butter

1 tsp (5 mL) lemon zest

1/4 cup (60 mL) fresh lemon juice (2 lemons)

Chopped parsley, for garnish

Lemon wedges, for serving

HOW TO

Preheat oven to 250°F (120°C).

Combine flour with salt and pepper to taste in a large shallow plate. Pat sole fillets dry with paper towels.

Heat 1 tbsp (15 mL) of the oil in a large sauté pan over medium-high heat. Add 1 tbsp (15 mL) butter and quickly swirl. Dredge 2 sole fillets in the seasoned flour on both sides, carefully shaking off excess, and place them in the hot pan. Cook for 2 minutes or until fish loosens from the pan and is lightly golden underneath. Add half the lemon zest and half the lemon juice, then turn fish carefully with a thin spatula. Cook for 2 minutes on the other side.

As soon as fish is cooked through, carefully transfer to warm plates and keep fish warm in the oven while you repeat the process with the remaining 2 fillets.

Sprinkle with salt and pepper and serve immediately with lemon wedges and a good sprinkle of chopped parsley and lemon zest. (I have sometimes omitted the parsley—a classic ingredient for this dish—because the green flecks threw off the kids, but please add liberally!)

Serve with steamed rice and your favourite vegetable. I love this fish with grilled asparagus or grilled radicchio.

....

Kitchen Notes: Always ask at the fish counter when the fish came in—ideally, you want same day.

Variations: If you want a little crunch, mix 1/2 cup (125 mL) panko bread crumbs in with the flour. You can also add a little Parmesan.

You can make a quick sauce in the same pan, melting 2 tbsp (30 mL) butter and swirling in parsley and lemon juice to taste; pour over the fish.

Swap sole for another light white fish such as tilapia. Ask your fishmonger for local lake fish such as trout.

Lake of the Woods Cheater Salt-and-Vinegar Chips Fish Fry

Elena, my behind-the-scenes pro tester, told me about a dead easy fish fry from the Kawarthas: "Catch a bass from the lake, clean and fillet it, crunch up a bag of salt-and-vinegar chips, drop fish in bag, shake it, then fry it!" My mom grew up on Lake of the Woods with my friend Tori Newall's mom, whose fish fry was very similar, although her local fish is pickerel. Try it!

SERVES 6

INGREDIENTS

6 local fish fillets (pickerel, bass, trout)
1 large bag salt-and-vinegar chips
1 lemon, cut into wedges

HOW TO

"Go fishing," says Elena.

Pat fish dry with paper towels.

Crush bag of chips in the bag (eat a few before!) so they resemble coarse bread crumbs. Shake fillets in bag of crushed chips. Set fish aside on a plate.

Heat a large nonstick or cast-iron frying pan over medium-high heat. (You won't need to use any oil because of the oil in the chips.) Fry fish 1 to 2 minutes per side (depending on thickness) or until crust is brown and fish is just cooked. Serve with lemon wedges.

....

Kitchen Notes: To crush the chips, open the bag to let the air out, then run a rolling pin over them. Or put them in a mini food processor and give them a few whirs until they resemble coarse bread crumbs.

Variations: Try salt-and-black-pepper chips—or experiment!
You can use tilapia, but since it will have been frozen it will be a bit dry, so use an egg to help the coating stick. Whisk 1 egg, dip fillets in egg, then shake in the chip bag. Fry in 1 tsp (5 mL) vegetable oil.

Greek-Style Chicken on a Stick with Grilled Pita

The kids love most things "on a stick" and all things "make yourself" since they get to choose what they like. I guess the radishes are for adults only.

SERVES 4

INGREDIENTS

4 large boneless skinless chicken breasts, cut into large cubes
4 pitas
Tzatziki (recipe follows, or store-bought is fine)
Feta cheese, cubed and grilled (see Kitchen Notes below)
Chopped lettuce
Sliced cucumbers
8 radishes, sliced
Red onions pickled in lime juice (see Kitchen Notes below)

MARINADE

Zest of 1 lemon
2 tbsp (30 mL) fresh lemon juice (1 lemon)
3 tbsp (50 mL) olive oil
2 tbsp (30 mL) plain yogurt
1 tsp (5 mL) pepper
1/4 tsp (1 mL) cinnamon
1/4 tsp (1 mL) ground allspice
2 cloves garlic, minced (1 tsp/5 mL)

HOW TO

In a medium bowl, whisk together all marinade ingredients. Add chicken and toss to coat. Cover and refrigerate at least 30 minutes or up to 5 hours.

Soak 8 wooden skewers in water for at least 1 hour.

Preheat grill to medium-high. Thread chicken cubes onto skewers. Grill skewers 8 to 10 minutes or until juices run clear, turning every 2 minutes. Grill pitas until just warm, about 30 seconds per side.

Using a fork, slide chicken off skewers. Open pitas and fill with chicken, tzatziki, feta (or serve alongside), lettuce, cucumbers, radishes and pickled red onions (or chopped tomatoes and sweet peppers in a lemon vinaigrette).

Serve with Greek Vegetable Salad (page 58), couscous and more tzatziki.

Kitchen Notes: Make sure you soak wooden skewers in water to prevent burning.
You can also use 12-inch (30 cm) metal skewers.
To pickle red onions, slice very thin and cover in lime juice (or white vinegar) for 12 to 24 hours.
To grill feta, cut into large cubes, brush with olive oil and cook in a hot grill pan just until it turns brown and you get grill marks, about 5 minutes.
Greek staples: lemons, yogurt, garlic, oregano, feta, olives, onions.

Tzatziki

MAKES 1 CUP (250 ML)

INGREDIENTS

1 cup (250 mL) plain yogurt

1/2 English cucumber, peeled

1 clove garlic, minced

2 tsp (10 mL) fresh lemon juice

Salt and pepper to taste

HOW TO

Place yogurt in a bowl. Coarsely grate cucumber on a box grater right onto a clean tea towel; squeeze out excess liquid. Add cucumber to yogurt. Stir in garlic and lemon juice and season well.

Thai Chicken on a Stick
with Peanut Sauce

When it comes to ordering in, Thai is top of my list. But some Thai dishes—like this one—are so simple to whip up, you don't have to pick up the phone. It's all about stocking the pantry with key ingredients like coconut milk, fish sauce and curry paste.

MAKES 20 TO 24 SATAYS

INGREDIENTS

1 can (14 oz/398 mL) light coconut milk

Zest and juice of 1 lime

4 tsp (20 mL) fish sauce

2 tbsp (30 mL) crushed peanuts (optional)

2 tsp (10 mL) brown sugar

1 tsp (5 mL) red curry paste

4 tsp (20 mL) chopped fresh cilantro or basil

1 green onion, thinly sliced

2 cloves garlic, minced

1 tsp (5 mL) salt

1/2 tsp (2 mL) pepper

2 lb (1 kg) boneless skinless chicken breasts, cut into large strips

HOW TO

Soak 24 bamboo skewers in water for at least 1 hour.

In a large bowl, combine coconut milk, lime zest and juice, fish sauce, peanuts (if using), brown sugar, curry paste, cilantro, green onion, garlic, salt and pepper. Add chicken and toss to coat. Refrigerate up to 4 hours.

Preheat grill to medium-high.

Thread chicken strips onto soaked skewers, pushing tightly together. Lightly grease grill (or heat a grill pan over medium-high heat). Grill skewers, turning once, 5 to 7 minutes per side or until chicken is no longer pink inside.

Serve with peanut sauce (next page), a few squirts of lime, steamed jasmine rice and store-bought shrimp chips. The London Mango Salad (page 65) is a perfect complement.

....

Kitchen Notes: Thai pantry essentials: fish sauce, curry paste (red, green or yellow depending on heat factor), coconut milk, vermicelli noodles, limes, shrimp chips.

Variation: Substitute crushed almonds for the peanuts.

Peanut Sauce

MAKES 2 1/2 CUPS (625 ML)

INGREDIENTS

1 tbsp (15 mL) vegetable oil

2 cloves garlic, crushed

2 tsp (10 mL) red curry paste

1 can (14 oz/398 mL) light coconut milk

1/4 cup (60 mL) brown sugar

1/4 cup (60 mL) fresh lemon juice

1 1/2 cups (375 mL) ground peanuts or chunky peanut butter

Salt and pepper

HOW TO

In a medium saucepan, heat oil over medium heat. Add garlic and cook, stirring, until just golden. Add curry paste and cook, stirring, for 2 minutes. Add coconut milk and sugar. Bring to a boil, reduce heat and simmer for 10 to 15 minutes or until thickened.

Stir in lemon juice. Add peanuts and simmer, stirring occasionally, until the sauce begins to thicken. Season to taste with salt and pepper. Let cool.

....

Variations: Turn this into an almond sauce by replacing ground peanuts with ground almonds or almond butter.

This is delicious in a mock pad thai: In a frying pan over medium heat, toss the peanut sauce with softened vermicelli noodles, a whisked egg, veggies like bean sprouts, red pepper and some puréed tomatoes, and fish sauce, sugar and lime juice to taste. Sprinkle with chopped green onion.

Korean Chicken Thighs

One of my seasoned recipe testers, Stewie, got this recipe from a next-door neighbour's Korean grandmother. She freezes the thighs right in the marinade if she doesn't have time to cook them. They are great to have on hand for lunches or a quick dinner.   **SERVES 4 TO 6**

INGREDIENTS

3 lb (1.5 kg) boneless skinless chicken thighs (about 12 pieces)

MARINADE

1/3 cup (75 mL) soy sauce
1/4 cup (60 mL) Japanese rice wine (sake)
1/4 cup (60 mL) water
3 tbsp (50 mL) sesame oil
3 tbsp (50 mL) packed brown sugar
1 tbsp (15 mL) minced fresh ginger
1/2 tsp (2 mL) Chinese hot sauce
3 cloves garlic, minced
Freshly ground pepper to taste

HOW TO

Clean and pat dry chicken thighs; place in a large resealable plastic bag. In a medium bowl, whisk together all marinade ingredients. Add to chicken and marinate, refrigerated, for 24 hours, turning periodically.
Preheat grill to medium-high.
Remove chicken from marinade (discard marinade) and grill 15 minutes or until cooked through and juices run clear. Don't overcook.

....

Kitchen Notes: You can also do these in the oven. Preheat oven to 425°F (220°C). Roast 25 minutes or until the juices run clear.

Chicken Drumettes

These are great for a movie-night kitchen-counter dinner with Baked Sweet Potato Fries (page 174) and Caesar Salad (page 51). Kids love to grab hold and dig in.

SERVES 4

INGREDIENTS

1/2 cup (125 mL) ketchup

1/4 cup (60 mL) Worcestershire sauce

2 tbsp (30 mL) soy sauce

2 tbsp (30 mL) brown sugar

2 tbsp (30 mL) minced garlic

2 tbsp (30 mL) toasted sesame seeds

2 tsp (10 mL) sambal oelek

2 lb (1 kg) chicken drumettes

HOW TO

In a bowl, stir together ketchup, Worcestershire sauce, soy sauce, brown sugar, garlic, sesame seeds and sambal oelek. Add chicken and toss to coat. Put into a resealable plastic bag and marinate, refrigerated, for at least 3 hours or up to 1 day, turning occasionally.

Preheat oven to 375°F (190°C). Line a baking sheet with foil and place a rack on top.

Remove chicken from marinade (discard marinade) and place on rack. Bake for 25 to 30 minutes or until chicken is no longer pink and juices run clear.

Serve hot or at room temperature with your favourite dipping sauce, such as blue cheese or ranch.

....

Kitchen Notes: Sambal oelek is an Asian chili sauce available widely in supermarkets and specialty stores. You can substitute sweet chili sauce, which is less hot.

Variations: You can use chicken wingettes instead of drumettes. You can even use thighs or breasts. You can grill these instead of baking. Heat grill to medium and lightly oil the rack. Remove excess marinade from chicken (to prevent burning), and grill, turning once or twice, for 25 to 30 minutes or until juices run clear.

This marinade is also great with beef short ribs.

Mom's Zephyr Island Barbecued Pineapple Chicken

This is one of the most popular summer cottage meals in our family. Great for making ahead, serving a crowd and eating the leftovers cold. It's perfect for picnics, and the kids love it!

SERVES 8 TO 10

INGREDIENTS

18 pieces bone-in chicken (thighs, drumsticks, breasts)

Salt and pepper to taste

1 1/4 cups (300 mL) brown sugar

3/4 cup (175 mL) soy sauce

1 tsp (5 mL) ground ginger

2 cloves garlic, peeled, halved and smashed

2 cups (500 mL) crushed pineapple with juice (from a 19-oz/540 mL can)

HOW TO

Preheat oven to 400°F (200°C).

Wash chicken, pat dry and sprinkle with salt and pepper.

In a medium bowl, whisk together brown sugar, soy sauce, ginger and garlic. Stir in crushed pineapple. Divide marinade between two 9- x 13-inch (3 L) baking dishes. Add chicken, flipping a few times to coat.

Bake, covered, for 35 to 40 minutes or until juices run clear. Do not overcook. Turn chicken pieces over, then cool completely. Cover and refrigerate 24 hours.

Preheat grill to medium-high.

Remove chicken from marinade and discard marinade. Grill chicken 5 minutes per side or until you have nice grill marks and chicken is warmed through.

Serve with coleslaw (page 69) and rice.

....

Kitchen Notes: I would love to encourage you to use fresh pineapple, but the canned with its juices is better.

You can use boneless thighs and breasts, but you'll be compromising a bit of the tenderness and flavour. If using boneless breasts, reduce baking time to about 20 minutes or until juices run clear. Do not overcook.

Chicken and Broccoli Casserole

My mom (and Bryce's mom and many other moms I know) made a simpler version of this old-fashioned comfort pantry dish when I was growing up—chicken and a can of cream of mushroom or chicken soup. It became a university staple. We still love it, and our kids love it, but I felt inclined to dress it up, if you can call it that.

SERVES 4

INGREDIENTS

1 can (10 oz/284 mL) cream of mushroom soup

1 cup (250 mL) sour cream or plain yogurt

4 bone-in chicken breasts with skin (excess fat removed if necessary)

1 cup (250 mL) chopped cremini mushrooms (about 7 medium)

1/2 cup (125 mL) grated aged white Cheddar cheese

1/2 cup (125 mL) dry bread crumbs

1 bunch broccoli, cut into small florets

HOW TO

Preheat oven to 350°F (180°C).

Stir together cream of mushroom soup and sour cream.

In a lightly greased casserole dish, arrange chicken breasts skin side up. Scatter mushrooms over chicken. Pour soup mixture over top and spread evenly.

Bake, uncovered, for 25 minutes or until beginning to bubble.

Meanwhile, in a small bowl, mix cheese and bread crumbs.

In a medium pot of boiling salted water, blanch broccoli 1 minute or until bright green. Drain.

Remove casserole from oven. Carefully top with broccoli and sprinkle with bread crumb topping. Bake for another 20 minutes or until bubbling and golden.

Serve over rice.

....

Kitchen Notes: My mom never buys boneless skinless chicken breasts. She says they are always dry and lack flavour.

My grandmother Bo would simmer chicken on the bone in a pot of water with chopped onion, chopped celery, peppercorns and a bay leaf for a delicious poached chicken, equally comforting and just as easy.

Mock Butter Chicken

My favourite dish to order in is Butter Chicken from Rashna, a Sri Lankan restaurant in Cabbagetown. I ordered it so often that it got to the point that when I called, before I could even place my order the owner would say, "Twenty minutes." Our son, Fin, loved it from a very early age, and now all our kids love the heat and the depth of flavour. My recipe is a mock version, reducing the lengthy ingredients list and process while still maintaining the deep Indian flavours. The key is to simmer this dish low and slow, giving the flavours time to meld.

SERVES 4

INGREDIENTS

3 tbsp (50 mL) butter

2 tsp (10 mL) cumin seeds

1 medium Vidalia onion, finely chopped

2 cloves garlic, minced

1 tsp (5 mL) minced fresh ginger

2 tsp (10 mL) garam masala

1 tsp (5 mL) cayenne, or to taste

1 tsp (5 mL) ground coriander

1/4 cup (60 mL) ground almonds

2 lb (1 kg) boneless skinless chicken thighs, cut into 2-inch (5 cm) chunks

1 1/2 cups (325 mL) canned tomato purée

1/2 cup (125 mL) 35% cream

1/2 cup (125 mL) Balkan-style plain yogurt

HOW TO

In a large heavy sauté pan, melt butter over medium heat. Fry cumin seeds for 1 minute or until fragrant. Add onion and fry until translucent, about 3 minutes. Add garlic, ginger, garam masala, cayenne, coriander and ground almonds. Cook, stirring, for 2 minutes or until fragrant.

Add chicken pieces and toss to coat with onion and spices. Fry, stirring frequently, until chicken is nearly cooked through, about 5 minutes.

Add tomato purée and cream; bring to a boil, stirring. Reduce heat to low and simmer, uncovered, 15 minutes. Cover and continue to simmer another 10 to 15 minutes or until sauce is slightly thickened. Remove from heat and stir in yogurt.

Serve over basmati rice, with warmed naan bread (store-bought naan, wrapped in foil and warmed in the oven, will do the trick) and raita (store-bought, or homemade: mix yogurt, garlic, cucumber and lemon) for dipping.

....

Kitchen Notes: This dish has a mild heat that is perfect for adults and kids who like just a bit of spice, but if you are feeding people who prefer their spices really mild, reduce the cayenne a bit. If you want to add heat, increase cayenne or add a red chili, split lengthwise, with the onion at the start. Remove chili at the end.

I have made this dish using ground cumin instead of whole cumin seeds, and it was delicious.

For people with nut allergies, you can leave out the almonds without compromising the flavour.

Chicken with Morels

This is adapted from a recipe in *Barefoot in Paris* by Ina Garten. I love the flavours and richness of French food, but I often reduce the fat content without compromising the flavour. I served this to my friends Ghislaine and Tony one night. Ghislaine, a great cook, usually does the hosting. Tony said, "Wow, you really can cook!" I guess I owed them a few dinners! This is a perfect special comfort dinner that says "thank you."

SERVES 6

INGREDIENTS

1 oz (30 g) dried morels

6 small boneless skinless chicken breasts

Salt and pepper

Flour, for dredging

1/4 cup (60 mL) vegetable oil

2 large shallots, finely chopped (about 1/4 cup/60 mL)

2 cloves garlic, minced

1 cup (250 mL) Madeira

2 cups (500 mL) chicken stock

1 cup (250 mL) whipping cream

Juice of 1/2 lemon (about 2 tbsp/30 mL)

2 tbsp (30 mL) chopped chives

2 tbsp (30 mL) chopped parsley

HOW TO

Preheat oven to 400°F (200°C).

Soak morels in hot water for 30 minutes. Lift morels carefully from the water and rinse well to remove all the grittiness. Discard liquid and dry morels on paper towels. Set aside.

Sprinkle chicken with salt and pepper. Dredge in flour and shake off the excess.

Heat half the oil in a large sauté pan over medium heat. Cook chicken in 2 batches until browned on both sides, about 5 minutes per side. Transfer chicken as it's cooked to a casserole dish.

Add the rest of the oil to the pan. Add morels, shallots and garlic. Cook for 2 minutes, stirring constantly. Increase heat to high. Pour Madeira into the pan and reduce the liquid by half, about 2 minutes. Add chicken stock, cream, lemon juice, and salt and pepper to taste. Boil until the sauce starts to thicken, about 5 minutes. Pour the sauce over the chicken.

Bake for 10 minutes or until the chicken is heated through. Garnish with chives and parsley.

Serve over egg noodles with a simple green salad.

....

Kitchen Notes: If you have trouble finding morels, you can substitute dried porcini mushrooms.

Coq au Vin

When I started teaching cooking classes, I enjoyed sharing my love for French comfort food and my memories of happy times in France. The students had fun making this classic but easy dish—it made them feel like true French chefs. Make this on a weekend when you have time to enjoy the whole experience, and enjoy with a bottle of your favourite Burgundy or Bordeaux.

SERVES 6 TO 8

INGREDIENTS

3 stalks celery, coarsely chopped

2 medium carrots, sliced

2 onions, coarsely chopped

6 large sprigs fresh thyme

2 bay leaves

1 bottle (750 mL) plus 1/2 cup (125 mL) dry red wine

6 chicken legs

1 1/2 cups (375 mL) pearl onions

5 tbsp (80 mL) butter, at room temperature

12 oz (375 g) large mushrooms, quartered

4 slices bacon, chopped

Salt and pepper to taste

1 tbsp (15 mL) vegetable oil

1/2 cup (125 mL) port

1/2 cup (125 mL) chicken stock

2 tbsp (30 mL) all-purpose flour

2 tbsp (30 mL) butter

HOW TO

In a large heavy non-aluminum pot, combine celery, carrots, onions, thyme, bay leaves and the bottle of wine. Cut chicken legs at the joint into thighs and drumsticks. Add chicken to pot, submerging completely. Cover and refrigerate overnight.

Bring a large pot of salted water to a boil. Add pearl onions and cook for 3 minutes. Drain and cool. Peel. (The skins will slip right off.)

In a large heavy frying pan over medium-high heat, melt 3 tbsp (50 mL) of the butter until foam subsides. Add pearl onions and mushrooms; sauté until mushrooms are tender, about 10 minutes. Transfer to a bowl. Add bacon to same pan and sauté until brown and crisp. Transfer bacon to paper towels to drain. Wipe pan clean.

Using a slotted spoon, transfer chicken pieces to a strainer (reserve marinade in pot). Pat chicken dry with paper towels; sprinkle with salt and pepper.

Heat vegetable oil in same pan over medium-high heat. Add chicken and sauté until skin is brown, turning once, about 10 minutes.

Return chicken to pot of marinade. Bring to a boil, reduce heat and simmer, uncovered, until chicken is very tender, about 1 hour and 15 minutes.

Strain chicken and cooking liquid over a large bowl. Transfer chicken to bowl with mushrooms; discard vegetables in strainer. Return liquid to pot. Add port, chicken stock and remaining 1/2 cup (125 mL) wine; bring to a boil.

Combine flour and remaining 2 tbsp (30 mL) butter in a small bowl, mashing with the back of a small spoon. Whisk into cooking liquid bit by bit. Boil over medium heat until sauce thickens and is slightly reduced, about 15 minutes. Add chicken, pearl onions, mushrooms and bacon. Simmer, stirring occasionally, until chicken is heated through and flavours blend, about 10 minutes.

Serve over egg noodles.

....

Kitchen Notes: Ask your butcher to cut the chicken legs into thighs and drumsticks and you're ready to go. Or buy thighs and drumsticks separately.

You can buy frozen peeled pearl onions—so easy, and no one will be the wiser!

Jamaican Shediac Cape Curry

This recipe comes from Jen Fraser, a TV food producer and fellow Cabbagetowner. It was taught to her by her friend Delano, who was born in Jamaica and whose style of cooking was aromatic and flavourful. This is Jen's variation on his classic. It has become a summer cottage staple in Shediac Cape, New Brunswick, where Jen makes it using fresh vegetables and herbs from her dad's garden.

SERVES 4 OR 5

INGREDIENTS

1 tbsp (15 mL) vegetable oil

2 cups (500 mL) chicken (4 to 5 breasts or thighs) cut into bite-size pieces

Salt and pepper to taste

1 large onion, finely chopped

1 or 2 cloves garlic, minced

2 to 3 tbsp (30 to 50 mL) curry powder (mild or hot depending on how you like it)

1 tsp (5 mL) ground cumin

1/2 tsp (2 mL) dried thyme

1 can (14 oz/398 mL) coconut milk

1 1/4 cups (300 mL) good-quality chicken stock

1 to 2 carrots, sliced

1/2 cup (125 mL) chopped sweet potato

1/2 cup (125 mL) fresh or frozen peas

2 tbsp (30 mL) chopped fresh cilantro

HOW TO

In a Dutch oven or large heavy saucepan, heat oil over medium heat. Season chicken with salt and pepper. Brown chicken for 4 to 5 minutes. Transfer to a plate.

Add onion and garlic to pot and cook, stirring frequently, until onion is translucent. Add curry powder, cumin and thyme; cook, stirring, until fragrant, 1 to 2 minutes.

Add coconut milk and chicken stock, stirring to scrape up any brown bits and making sure all spices are dissolved. Add carrots, sweet potato and chicken; simmer for 30 to 45 minutes or until carrots and sweet potato are a bit soft.

Add peas and 1 tbsp (15 mL) of the cilantro; simmer for another 3 to 5 minutes, until vegetables are tender but peas are still bright green. Add salt and pepper to taste.

Serve on a bed of rice, garnished with remaining cilantro. Serve with mango chutney and yogurt.

....

Kitchen Notes: This curry is delicious served with coconut-flavoured yogurt. The yogurt will help mellow the heat for those who like their curry really mild.

No-Fail Roast Chicken

A roast chicken is a special-occasion family favourite at my mom's and grandmother's tables. I love this for Sunday dinner; it sets us up for Monday sandwiches and salads. **SERVES 6 TO 8**

INGREDIENTS

1 lemon, cut in half

1 roasting chicken (4 to 5 lb/2 to 2.2 kg), rinsed and patted dry

Kosher salt and pepper to taste

2 or 3 sprigs fresh rosemary or thyme

3 stalks celery, tops and leaves only

1/2 onion

1 to 2 tbsp (15 to 30 mL) plus 1 tbsp (15 mL) butter

FOR THE GRAVY

3 tbsp (50 mL) all-purpose flour

1 1/2 cups (375 mL) good-quality chicken stock

HOW TO

Preheat oven to 425°F (220°C).

Sprinkle chicken cavity liberally with salt and pepper. Place lemon halves, herbs, celery tops and leaves, and onion in cavity. Rub chicken all over with 1 to 2 tbsp (15 to 30 mL) butter. Sprinkle liberally with salt and pepper. Place chicken in a small roasting pan or 12-inch (30 cm) cast-iron frying pan.

Roast chicken, uncovered and basting several times, about 1 1/2 hours. Juices should run clear, and a sharp knife inserted between the thigh and the breast should come out hot; a meat thermometer inserted in the thigh close to the body should read 170°F (75°C).

Transfer chicken to a cutting board and tent loosely with foil. Let rest while you make the gravy.

Spoon fat from the roasting pan, leaving about 4 tbsp (60 mL). Place roasting pan over medium heat (you may need to use two burners). Stir up any browned bits in the pan to help the browning. Add a pinch of sugar if you wish. Sprinkle in flour, stirring constantly, and cook 5 minutes or until the flour is light brown. Turn up heat and add chicken broth, stirring constantly. Bring to a boil, then reduce heat and simmer, stirring frequently, 5 to 10 minutes or until desired consistency. Season with salt and pepper. Stir in remaining 1 tbsp (15 mL) butter and simmer for 1 more minute. Serve with the chicken. Mashed potatoes (page 176) are a must.

....

Kitchen Notes: A 3- to 4-lb (1.5 to 2 kg) chicken takes 1 hour and 15 minutes to cook and serves 4. It will not yield as much fat for the gravy; you won't need to pour off the excess.

Thanksgiving or Christmas Turkey

For approaching forty years, my mom, my mother-in-law or one of my grandmothers has cooked our Christmas (and Thanksgiving) turkey dinner. Even though I have hosted more than a few Christmas dinners, my mom or mother-in-law either brings the turkey ready to go or comes over and helps with (that is, does) the turkey prep. My dad is usually at the ready, like a surgeon's assistant just scrubbed up, to help lift the beast, stuff and truss it. It's always best (and most relaxing) if I just stay out of the way. But this year I will grow up and do it all myself.

SERVES 10 TO 14 WITH LEFTOVERS

INGREDIENTS
1 turkey (12 to 16 lb/5.5 to 7.2 kg)

Salt and pepper to taste

1/4 cup (60 mL) butter, at room temperature

BASIC BREAD STUFFING
4 cups (1 L) chunky bread crumbs (stale bread pulsed in the food processor or, if store-bought, as chunky as possible)

2 or 3 stalks celery, finely chopped

3 or 4 green onions, finely chopped

1/4 cup (60 mL) chopped parsley

2 tsp (10 mL) poultry seasoning

1 tsp (5 mL) dried sage

Salt and pepper to taste

1/3 cup (75 mL) butter, melted

1 cup (250 mL) chicken stock or water (approx)

HOW TO
Preheat oven to 325°F (160°C).

Clear the sink and counter of dishes. Remove giblets, neck and gizzards from the cavity of the bird. Put them in a small pot and cover with water; set aside. Wash the bird inside and out with cold running water. Pat dry with paper towels. Salt the inside of the bird.

To make the stuffing, in a medium bowl, combine bread crumbs, celery, green onions, parsley, poultry seasoning, sage, salt and pepper; stir with a fork. Slowly drizzle in butter, stirring with a fork. Drizzle in chicken stock until the stuffing holds together (this is when you need to lightly use your hands).

Stuff bird with stuffing in both ends—neck cavity and body cavity. Pull the neck skin over the stuffing and fasten with a skewer. Push together the back opening and skewer shut as well. Tuck in legs and tie with string.

Place turkey breast side up in a lightly greased shallow roasting pan (no more than 2 inches/ 5 cm tall). Rub all over with butter and sprinkle with salt and pepper. Tent turkey loosely with foil.

Roast turkey for 3 3/4 to 4 hours total. After the first hour, remove foil and baste turkey. Return to oven (without foil) and roast, basting occasionally with pan drippings to help brown turkey, until an instant-read thermometer in the thickest part of the thigh reads just shy of 175 to 180°F (80 to 85°C). (The turkey will continue to cook a little out of the oven.) Remove turkey from the oven, tent loosely with foil and allow it to rest for 20 minutes before carving.

Meanwhile, bring pot with giblets to a low boil and cook for at least 1 hour. Set aside to use water for gravy.

Make gravy according to the instructions on page 117, using water from giblets instead of potato water.

Turkey Tips

My mom has great debates (primarily with herself) about fresh versus organic versus free-range versus frozen. She even contemplates doing two smaller capons instead of one big bird. For lots of people, a frozen Butterball does the trick.

We have cooked stuffing both inside and outside the bird, and despite recent high-profile chefs' recipes for baking it outside the bird, in our family of a dozen seasoned turkey eaters, the vote was unanimous—stuffing is best baked inside the bird.

The size of bird should depend on the number of guests. Allow for 3/4 to 1 lb (375 to 500 g) per person and 1 lb+ (500 g+) per person if you're counting on generous leftovers.

To thaw a turkey in the fridge, allow 5 hours per pound (500 g). An 8- to 10-lb (3.5 to 4.5 kg) frozen bird will take 2 days to thaw in the fridge.

Roasting times

The larger the bird, the fewer number of minutes are needed per pound.

For a stuffed bird, at 325°F (160°C):
10 to 12 lb (4.5 to 5.5 kg): 3 1/2 to 3 3/4 hours
12 to 16 lb (5.5 to 7.2 kg): 3 3/4 to 4 hours
16 to 22 lb (7.2 to 10 kg): 4 to 4 1/2 hours

When the turkey is ready, an instant-read thermometer inserted in the thickest part of the thigh should read 180°F (85°C).

Let the bird rest at least 20 minutes before carving.

FIN'S   dinners

1. Risotto - plain
2. Spagetti - Pesto
3. Sole - fish
4. Wifesaver
5. Lamb chops
6. Tacos
7. Pizza
8. Spanokopita

Mains
[meats]

Grilled T-Bone Steak with Horseradish

Grill-Pan Rib-Eye with Creamy Mushrooms

Helen Ducklin's Beef Stroganoff

Miami-Style Barbecued Beef Short Ribs

Winter Beef Bourguignon

Stovetop Pot Roast and Noodles à la Lee

Sunday Roast Beef Dinner

Friday-Night Burgers

Mom's Meatloaf

Cottage Chili

Kristi's Mom's Brandy Beans

Virginia's Meatballs

Aunt Nancy's Dry-Rub Ribs

Ode-to-Ontario Pork Tenderloin

Baked Ham

Pork Chops on the Grill

Shannon and Elena's Southern Pulled Pork

Mustard-Crusted Rack of Lamb

Roast Leg of Lamb

Curried Lamb Leftovers

Grilled T-Bone Steak with Horseradish

A steak on the grill is a family favourite. It works as one meal at two different times when the kids eat at five and Bryce and I eat later. We fire up the barbecue snow or heat, so the steaming-hot baked potato accompaniment is a must in the winter months.

SERVES 2 TO 4

INGREDIENTS

1 1/2 lb (750 g) T-bone steak

1 tsp (5 mL) Worcestershire sauce

1 tsp (5 mL) dry mustard

1 tsp (5 mL) steak seasoning

Salt and pepper to taste

1/4 cup (60 mL) hot horseradish

2 tbsp (30 mL) Dijon mustard

2 tbsp (30 mL) sour cream

HOW TO

Bring steak to room temperature before grilling. Preheat grill to medium-high.

Season steak on both sides with Worcestershire sauce, dry mustard, steak seasoning and salt and pepper.

In a small bowl, combine horseradish, mustard and sour cream.

Grill steak 5 to 6 minutes per side or until gorgeously crusted and medium-rare.

Let steak rest 5 to 10 minutes, loosely tented with foil. Cut meat off the bone in two pieces and thinly slice steak on an angle against the grain.

Serve with creamy horseradish and, of course, baked potatoes.

....

Grill tips:

Bring meat to room temperature before grilling.

Keep your grill clean. Use a grill brush every time to clean the rack, and replace your brush often. Put the cover on once the barbecue has cooled, to prevent rusting.

Get to know your grill. Yours and your dad's are not the same—kind of like cars.

Grilling cuts:

T-bone: the bone keeps it tender, and you get part of the loin—the best of both worlds (as seen in photo).

Striploin: less fat; easy to cook and carve (off the bone); quicker grill time (5 minutes per side); may have less flavour with less fat.

Rib-eye: good fat marbling means lots of flavour.

Grill-Pan Rib-Eye with Creamy Mushrooms

We like to have a steak once a week—it's such an easy dinner. While I love to barbecue, it's nicer to not have to step outside when it's minus ten. Condo and apartment dwellers take note—all you need here is a grill pan.

SERVES 2

INGREDIENTS

1 rib-eye steak (12 oz /375 g)

Salt and pepper

1 tsp (5 mL) grapeseed oil

6 slices bacon, chopped

2 shallots, finely chopped

3 cloves garlic, chopped

1 lb (500 g) assorted mushrooms (cremini, shiitake, oyster), chopped

1/4 cup (60 mL) Madeira, or beef stock

1/4 cup (60 mL) 35% cream (optional)

Chopped fresh thyme to taste

HOW TO

Bring steak to room temperature. Season steak generously with salt and pepper.

Heat a seasoned cast-iron or other heavy frying pan on medium-high. (Turn on the fan.) If using cast iron, you can sauté in a dry pan, without any oil. Otherwise, add a drop of grapeseed oil.

Grill steak, without moving or lifting it, about 4 minutes depending on thickness or until it doesn't stick and a nice crust has formed. Flip once and continue to grill to desired doneness, about 4 minutes more for medium-rare. Transfer to a plate and tent with foil.

In the same pan, sauté bacon until nice and crisp. Drain on paper towels.

Remove fat from pan, leaving about 1 tbsp (15 mL). Add shallots and sauté 1 to 2 minutes, until translucent. Add garlic and sauté another minute. Add mushrooms and sauté for another 5 minutes. Return bacon to pan.

Add Madeira or stock, cream if using, and steak juices that have accumulated on the plate. Season with thyme, salt and pepper. Simmer until reduced by half.

Slice steak on an angle against the grain. Serve sauce over the steak.

....

Kichen Notes: This is delicious with grilled or roasted red peppers or succotash (page 61).

Meat cooked on the barbecue, in a pan or in the oven can cook up to 10°F (5°C) more after it's removed from the heat. That's why cooked meat should always be given a rest—to finish cooking and to help the meat retain the juices for maximum tenderness. Better to pull it off a little before it's done and let it come to the perfect temperature. If you fear you have overcooked it, get it out of the hot pan and pour your guests a glass of wine!

Variations: If this feels too high fat or one step too many, drop the bacon.

Helen Ducklin's Beef Stroganoff

Helen is a great friend of my grandma Dodie's. They used to ski together and loved to entertain friends. Helen and her husband, Arnold, came to lots of family gatherings at my grandparents' place, and I always remember Helen trudging through the snow with dishes in hand.
This is a perfect après-ski dinner on a cold night.   **SERVES 4 TO 6**

INGREDIENTS

3 tbsp (50 mL) all-purpose flour

Salt and pepper to taste

1/2 cup (125 mL) butter

3 1/2 lb (1.75 kg) top-round steak, cut into 1-inch (2.5 cm) cubes

1 tsp (5 mL) chopped fresh thyme (or 1/2 tsp/2 mL dried)

1 onion, finely chopped

1 1/2 lb (750 g) cremini mushrooms, halved if small, quartered if large

1/2 cup (125 mL) beef stock

1 cup (250 mL) beer

1/2 cup (125 mL) tomato sauce

1 tsp (5 mL) Worcestershire sauce

2 cups (500 mL) sour cream

HOW TO

On a plate, mix flour, salt and pepper. Dredge beef in flour, shaking off excess.

In a Dutch oven or large heavy pot, melt butter over medium heat. Brown the meat in batches (do
   not overcrowd the pan). Transfer meat to a plate as it's cooked.

Stir thyme into pot. Stir in onion and cook until translucent, about 3 minutes, stirring from time to
   time. Stir in mushrooms and cook until soft, a few minutes. Return meat and any juices to the
   pot. Add beef stock, stirring and scraping up bits from bottom of pan. Stir in beer, tomato sauce
   and Worcestershire sauce. Cover, reduce heat and simmer for 1 1/2 hours or until meat is tender.

Stir in sour cream and season with salt and pepper.

Serve over egg noodles or rice.

....

Kitchen Notes: This dish uses a tender cut of meat and is finished with sour cream to give it
   a creamy consistency.

Miami-Style Barbecued Beef Short Ribs

This recipe has moved to the top of Fin's list of favourite dinners, replacing risotto. Call your butcher ahead of time, as these cuts are often available only in summer. Try this marinade on chicken drumettes.

SERVES 4

INGREDIENTS

4 lb (2 kg) Miami-style beef short ribs, 1 inch (2.5 cm) thick max,
  excess fat trimmed, or Korean short ribs, 1/2 inch (1 cm) thick

MARINADE

4 cloves garlic, minced

1/2 cup (125 mL) soy sauce

1/2 cup (125 mL) beer

1/4 cup (60 mL) honey

2 tbsp (30 mL) sesame oil

2 tsp (10 mL) sesame seeds

1 tsp (5 mL) minced fresh ginger
  (or 1/2 tsp/2 mL ground)

1 tsp (5 mL) Chinese chili paste or other
  hot sauce

6 green onions, chopped

HOW TO

Score fat side of ribs across the bone 1/2 inch (1 cm) deep.

In a bowl, whisk together garlic, soy sauce, beer, honey, sesame oil, sesame seeds, ginger and chili paste. Stir in green onions. Transfer ribs and marinade to a large resealable plastic bag. Marinate in fridge for 24 hours, turning occasionally.

Preheat grill to medium-high.

Remove ribs from marinade, reserving marinade. Place ribs meaty side down on grill, close lid and grill for 8 minutes (if using Miami-style ribs). Reduce heat to medium-low, flip ribs and grill, basting with reserved marinade, 6 more minutes or until ribs are brown and crisp. (If using Korean short ribs, grill on high 3 minutes per side.)

Serve with Wilted Spinach with Toasted Sesame Seeds (page 161) and Korean yam fries (page 174).

....

Kitchen Notes: Elena and I tested so many variations that we became beef short rib experts. Elena loves super-thin Korean ribs, while I prefer the 1-inch (2.5 cm) thick Miami cut. Korean short ribs are the thinnest (about 1/2 inch/1.25 cm thick), so you need 3 to 4 sides per person.

The regular 2-inch (5 cm) or thicker beef short ribs (like the ones pictured) are tough and need a long marinade and a slow cook. Increase marinating time to 48 to 72 hours. Add 1 cup (250 mL) more beer or beef stock and braise, uncovered, at 275°F (140°C) for 2 hours. Finish on the grill.

Korean staples: garlic, soy sauce, sesame oil, sesame seeds, ginger, chili paste.

Winter Beef Bourguignon

"As prepared in Burgundy" is the loose translation of "Bourguignon." I spent two years working for the travel company Butterfield & Robinson in Burgundy and I quickly learned that using some of the best red wine in the world made a pretty outstanding dish! When at home, always cook with a wine you would drink. The main ingredients of this classic (besides the beef!) are red wine, mushrooms and pearl onions. It's hearty and packed with flavour and perfect to make in the morning and enjoy that night.

SERVES 8 TO 10

INGREDIENTS

1/2 lb (250 g) bacon, diced

2 1/2 to 3 lb (1.25 to 1.5 kg) beef (top round, eye of round, or blade), cut into 1-inch (2.5 cm) cubes

Kosher salt and ground pepper to taste

1 tbsp (15 mL) olive oil

2 medium yellow onions, sliced

1 lb (500 g) carrots, cut into 1-inch (2.5 cm) chunks

1/2 lb (250 g) celery, finely chopped (4 stalks)

2 cloves garlic, chopped

3 tbsp (50 mL) all-purpose flour

1 1/2 cups (375 mL) red wine

1 cup (250 mL) port

1 tbsp (15 mL) tomato paste

2 cups (500 mL) beef stock (approx)

1 tsp (5 mL) chopped fresh thyme

2 tbsp (30 mL) butter, cubed

1 cup (250 mL) frozen pearl onions

1/2 lb (250 g) mushrooms, thickly sliced

HOW TO

Preheat oven to 250°F (120°C).

In a heavy pot or Dutch oven over medium heat, cook bacon until brown. Drain on paper towels. Reserve fat in pot.

Season beef with salt and pepper. Working in batches, brown the beef in bacon fat, transferring to a plate as it's browned. Discard bacon fat.

Add oil to pot. Add onions, carrots and celery; cook, stirring often, until light brown, about 10 minutes. Stir in garlic. Sprinkle with flour and stir for 5 minutes.

Increase heat to high. Add wine, stirring to scrape up bits from bottom of pan. Add port and reduce slightly. Turn heat down and stir in tomato paste. Return beef and any juices to pot and add enough stock to cover meat. Add thyme. Bring to a boil, cover and transfer to oven. Braise for 1 1/2 hours or until meat is tender.

Remove pot from oven and bring to a simmer on the stovetop. Stir in butter piece by piece until liquid starts to thicken. Add pearl onions and mushrooms; simmer, uncovered, 25 minutes or until vegetables are tender. Adjust seasonings and serve.

....

Kitchen Notes: Tough cuts require long, slow cooking to break down the tough meat and give you optimal tenderness. Blade is from the shoulder; top round and eye of round are leaner, from the hip.

Stovetop Pot Roast and Noodles à la Lee

This was a favourite when I was growing up—primarily for the gravy-soaked noodles and the slow-roasted onions. This dish defines comfort in a pot. You really do need a cast-iron Dutch oven for this and other slow-roast comfort foods.

SERVES 8

INGREDIENTS

1 boneless short rib, cross rib or blade roast
   (4 to 5 lb/2 to 2.2 kg), tied around middle

3 tbsp (50 mL) all-purpose flour, for browning

Salt and pepper to taste

2 tbsp (30 mL) vegetable oil

1/2 cup (125 mL) red wine (optional)

2 to 3 cups (500 to 750 mL) beef stock
   or water

8 extra-small onions, peeled

8 medium carrots, cut into large chunks

3 stalks celery, cut into large chunks

1 pkg (375 g) narrow egg noodles

FOR THE GRAVY

1/4 cup (60 mL) all-purpose flour

3/4 cup (175 mL) water

Salt and pepper

HOW TO

Pat meat dry with paper towel. Combine flour, salt and pepper on a plate and roll meat in it to lightly coat.

In a Dutch oven or large heavy pot, heat oil over medium heat. Brown meat well on all sides, about 15 minutes total.

Add wine if using and enough stock to go halfway up the side of the meat. Add water if necessary. Cover and bring to a boil. Reduce heat and simmer for 1 hour.

Add onions, carrots and celery around roast. Add more water or stock if necessary to cover vegetables. Cover and simmer for another 45 minutes to 1 hour or until vegetables are tender and meat nearly falls apart.

Remove roast and vegetables to a platter. Cover loosely with foil and let rest 15 minutes.

To make the gravy, in a small jar, shake flour and water together, ensuring there are no lumps. Put the pot over one or two burners and skim off fat, leaving about 4 tbsp (60 mL). Turn heat to medium. Slowly add flour mixture, stirring constantly with a wooden spoon, until thickened, 5 to 10 minutes. Season with salt and pepper.

Cook noodles according to package directions.

Remove string from roast. Slice meat very thinly. Serve meat and gravy over noodles, garnished with the vegetables.

Serve with Quick Fridge-Pickled Cucumbers (page 191) and Lee and Bo's Tomato Butter (page 186).

Sunday Roast Beef Dinner

In our family, my mom always said there was only one cut for Sunday dinner—a standing prime rib roast. My grandmother always asked the butcher for the first three or four ribs, depending how many chairs were at the table. (These ribs are the most flavourful.) I have vivid memories of roast beef with Yorkshire pudding as a Sunday norm—we didn't know how lucky we were.

SERVES 6 TO 8

INGREDIENTS

1 standing prime rib roast (5 to 6 lb/2.2 to 2.7 kg)

Salt and pepper to taste

2 tsp (10 mL) Worcestershire sauce

8 extra-small cooking onions, peeled

12 small potatoes, peeled

1/4 cup (60 mL) all-purpose flour

HOW TO

Bring meat to room temperature at least 1 hour before roasting. Set a rack at the second-lowest level and preheat oven to 475°F (240°C).

Season roast all over with salt and pepper. Rub with Worcestershire sauce. Place roast fat side up in a roasting pan and transfer to the oven.

Roast for 10 minutes, then turn temperature down to 350°F (180°C). Roast for 1 1/2 to 1 3/4 hours more, until an instant-read thermometer reads 130°F (55°C) for medium-rare. (Remember the meat will continue to cook out of the oven for up to 10°F/5°C.)

Meanwhile, in a medium pot, parboil potatoes and onions until slightly softened, about 10 minutes. Drain, reserving vegetable water for the gravy.

About an hour before the roast is done, place vegetables around the roast. If there is not a lot of fat in the pan, add a few teaspoons of bacon fat or vegetable oil before adding the vegetables.

Transfer roast to a carving board and let rest, covered with foil, at least 15 minutes while you make the gravy.

Pour off all but 3 to 4 tbsp (50 to 60 mL) fat from the pan. Place the pan over two burners and turn heat to medium. Slowly stir in flour, whisking constantly until flour is golden brown, about 5 minutes. Stirring constantly, slowly add 1 1/2 cups (375 mL) cooled water from cooking vegetables, scraping up the bits from the bottom of the pan. Simmer 5 minutes or until desired thickness. Taste before seasoning with salt and pepper.

To carve, remove the entire roast from the bone. Using a very sharp carving knife, carve into very thin slices. Serve immediately with the gravy and roast vegetables and, of course, with Yorkshire pudding (page 182).

Serve Quick Fridge-Pickled Cucumbers (page 191), fresh horseradish and hot mustard as accompaniments.

Kitchen Notes: Standing rib is simply a prime rib with the bones on. Ask your butcher to take the roast off the bones and then re-tie it—it'll be much easier to carve.

Letting the meat rest allows the juices to return to the centre of the meat, preserving its juiciness and tenderness.

Portions: allow for 1/2 lb (250 g) per person if the bone is left in and 1/3 lb (170 g) per person for a boned roast. A 5- to 6-lb (2.2 to 2.7 kg) bone-in roast serves 6 to 8, whereas a 5-lb (2.2 kg) boneless roast serves 8 to 10.

Other roasting cuts include sirloin tip, eye of round and rump roast. They're almost always sold without the bones, which makes them great for sandwiches the next day. But as with most meat, it's the bones and the fat that give it the flavour, so if you have the choice, go for the standing rib.

Friday-Night Burgers

Most Friday nights in the winter, my mom does burgers. My dad and Bryce could both barbe-cue 365 days a year, snowstorms and all. Our immediate family numbers twenty and counting, so when you are never sure who's arriving when, a platter of ready-to-grill burgers with a table full of fixings and a bowl of Bo's Coleslaw (page 69) is the perfect solution for staggered seat-ings. For me, it's all about the fixings!

MAKES 3 TO 6, DEPENDING ON WHETHER YOU MAKE QUARTER-POUNDERS OR HALF-POUNDERS

INGREDIENTS

1 1/2 lb (750 g) medium ground beef

1 egg

1 tbsp (15 mL) brown sugar

1 tbsp (15 mL) Worcestershire sauce

1 tbsp (15 mL) ketchup

1 tbsp (15 mL) prepared mustard

Salt and pepper to taste

3 to 6 slices aged Cheddar cheese

3 to 6 burger buns

HOW TO

In a large bowl, break up ground beef with your hands. Add egg, brown sugar, Worcestershire sauce, ketchup, mustard and salt and pepper; gently work in until incorporated.

Form 3 to 6 burgers about 1 inch (2.5 cm) thick. Do not overwork. Set aside on a plate lined with wax paper.

Fire up the grill to medium-high. Place burgers on grill for 4 minutes. Turn heat down to medium, flip burgers and cook second side another 5 minutes, laying cheese on top after 3 minutes. Adjust time based on your grill and desired doneness. In the last few minutes, warm buns on indirect heat on rack of grill.

Serve with coleslaw, all the fixings and your favourite chips.

....

Kitchen Notes: My mom has a couple of simple burger tips for success: use medium ground beef for flavour and worry not about the extra bit of fat in the name of good taste. Use soft fresh buns so the buns don't overpower the burger. She doesn't add brown sugar or Worcestershire, but I like the flavour they give.

Burgers can be made the morning of and kept refrigerated. You can even double your batch and freeze another night's worth.

Caramelized onions—slice 2 yellow onions and sauté low and slow in a cast-iron pan with a bit of butter until soft and deep golden, 15 to 20 minutes.

Sautéed mushrooms—slice and sauté in butter until soft and dark brown.

Bo's Good Mustard Sauce (page 188) or Bonnie's Mustard Pickles (page 192).

Chipotle ketchup—stir 1 chipotle from the can, chopped, into 1/2 cup (125 mL) ketchup.

Garlicky mayo—add 1 head of roasted garlic, squeezed out and chopped, to 1/2 cup (125 mL) mayo. To roast garlic, slice off a small piece from the top to expose the cloves, place whole head in foil, sprinkle with salt and pepper and a glug of good olive oil and roast at 375°F (190°C) for 30 minutes or until soft.

Grilled lettuces—cut radicchio or endive in half, brush with oil and grill for 1 to 2 minutes.

Cheeses—blue, Brie, aged or smoked Cheddar.

Ron's Buffalo Chicken Sliders

This is one of our friends Pauline and Ron's signature faves. This fun burger variation is perfect for casual gatherings—a quick alternative to a pulled pork party.   **SERVES 8**

INGREDIENTS

Meat from a whole roasted chicken, pulled into bite-size pieces

2 cups (500 mL) sour cream

2 cups (500 mL) crumbled blue cheese

2 stalks celery, diced

2 carrots, diced

HOW TO

Mix everything together and serve on toasted mini brioches with your favourite hot sauce.

Mom's Meatloaf

I am going to reveal a secret—the original recipe used Velveeta cheese. It was so moist and yummy that even non-meatloaf eaters were converted. I replaced the Velveeta with Cheddar cut into cubes, and it's just as moist—and yummier. **SERVES 6 TO 8**

INGREDIENTS

3/4 cup (175 mL) cubed aged Cheddar cheese
3/4 cup (175 mL) dry bread crumbs
1/2 cup (125 mL) finely chopped celery (2 stalks)
1/2 cup (125 mL) finely chopped sweet green pepper
1/2 cup (125 mL) finely chopped sweet red pepper
1/4 cup (60 mL) finely chopped onion
Salt and black pepper to taste
1 1/2 lb (750 g) lean ground beef
2 eggs
1 can (7 1/2 oz/213 mL) tomato sauce
2 tbsp (30 mL) ketchup

HOW TO

Preheat oven to 350°F (180°C).

In a large bowl, combine cheese, bread crumbs, celery, green and red peppers, onion and salt and black pepper. Pull apart ground beef and add to cheese-vegetable mixture.

In a small bowl, beat eggs with tomato sauce. Add to meat mixture and combine gently but thoroughly with your hands. Place in a loaf pan.

Bake for 45 minutes. Remove from oven and cover with ketchup. Bake 30 minutes more or until an instant-read thermometer reads 160°F (70°C).

Serve with baked potatoes.

....

Kitchen Notes: Divide the mixture in half and make 2 small loaves—bake one and freeze one. Sliced leftovers make for a delicious sandwich. In my days at dish café, Elena would have meatloaf sandwich day, and the men would come from miles. Load up your favourite bun with a thick slice of meatloaf, your favourite hot sauce or spicy ketchup and chipotle mayo.

Cottage Chili

This recipe is inspired by one in *The Cottage Cookbook*. Many a night on northern Georgian Bay, the winds are high, the air is cold, and the family gathers around for this delicious pot of cottage chili. The longer you simmer, the deeper the flavour. You can turn the heat off, then come back later and simmer again if it suits. The flavour is even better the next day.

SERVES 4 TO 6

INGREDIENTS

1 tbsp (15 mL) olive oil

1 cup (250 mL) chopped onion (1 medium)

3/4 cup (175 mL) chopped celery (about 2 stalks) (optional)

1 lb (500 g) lean ground beef

1 tsp (5 mL) salt

1 tbsp (15 mL) flour

1 cup (250 mL) chopped mushrooms

1 cup (250 mL) chopped sweet green pepper

1 tsp (5 mL) minced garlic (1 clove)

1 tbsp (15 mL) chili powder

2 cans (each 28 oz/796 mL) stewed tomatoes

2 cans (each 14 oz/398 mL) kidney beans, drained but not rinsed

Salt and black pepper to taste

HOW TO

In a large heavy pot, heat oil over medium-high heat. Add onion and sauté 2 minutes. Add celery if using and sauté another minute. Add ground beef, breaking it up with a wooden spoon. Sprinkle with salt and flour; brown the meat, stirring frequently, about 10 minutes.

Add mushrooms, green pepper and garlic; sauté a few minutes. Stir in chili powder, tomatoes and kidney beans. Reduce heat and simmer, stirring occasionally, 45 minutes or more. Season with salt and pepper.

Serve with warm crusty bread and a simple salad.

....

Kitchen Notes: Chili tastes best when it's cooked with a very low and long simmer. To minimize fuss, turn it on and off a few times to keep it cooking and continuing to concentrate the flavours. Turn it on while you do your jigsaw puzzle. Turn it off when you go dive in the lake. This freezes well. Cool completely before freezing. Better yet, double it for another family meal.

Kristi's Mom's Brandy Beans

Kristi and Rol and their kids showed up one year at my parents' farm during maple syrup production with warm Brandy Beans in hand. Kristi walked right into the sugar bush, put the bean pot on the fire during the maple syrup boil, and we all ate winter-camping-style. Each year come sap-running time, my dad hopes Kristi will arrive with lunch! **SERVES 8 TO 10**

INGREDIENTS

2 1b (1 kg) extra-lean ground beef

1 large onion, finely chopped

4 cloves garlic, minced

1/2 cup (125 mL) chili sauce

1/2 cup (125 mL) maple syrup

2 tsp (10 mL) dry mustard

1 tsp (5 mL) hot sauce

5 cans (each 14 oz/398 mL) baked brown beans in tomato sauce, drained

1/4 cup (60 mL) strong brewed coffee

1/4 cup (60 mL) brandy

HOW TO

Preheat oven to 350°F (180°C).

In a large heavy frying pan or Dutch oven over medium-high heat, brown the beef, breaking up with a wooden spoon. Drain off fat. Add onion and garlic to beef; sauté 5 minutes or until onion is light brown. Add chili sauce, maple syrup, mustard and hot sauce; mix well.

Layer beans and meat mixture in a casserole dish, beginning and ending with beans (3 layers of meat, 4 layers of beans). Top with coffee and brandy. Do not stir.

Bake, uncovered, for 30 to 40 minutes or until bubbly and brown.

....

Kitchen Notes: Baked beans come in many variations (with pork, in molasses and so on). I prefer the less-sweet baked beans in tomato sauce.

Variations: You can substitute ground turkey for ground beef, brown sugar for maple syrup, and dark rum for brandy.

Virginia's Meatballs

Virginia was my grandmother Bo's sister. I love how so many recipes still have the cook's name attached to them. My mom used to make these all the time when we were little—she would double the recipe and freeze a batch. The browning is a bit tedious but worth it, especially for the extra gravy on the baked potato.

MAKES 40 MEATBALLS

INGREDIENTS

2 lb (1 kg) ground round steak or lean ground beef

1 lb (500 g) lean ground pork

2 eggs, beaten

1/2 cup (125 mL) dry bread crumbs

1 tsp (5 mL) ground allspice

1 tsp (5 mL) salt

1 tsp (5 mL) pepper

Flour, for browning

2 tbsp (30 mL) vegetable oil

1 1/4 cups (300 mL) beef stock or water

HOW TO

In a large bowl, using a wooden spoon at first and then your hands, mix together ground steak, ground pork, eggs, bread crumbs, allspice, salt and pepper. Form 1-inch (2.5 cm) balls and roll lightly in flour.

In a large sauté pan, cast-iron pan or Dutch oven, heat oil over medium heat. Brown meatballs in batches, without crowding the pan, using tongs to turn meatballs so they brown evenly. Transfer meatballs to a plate as they're browned. Once they are all browned, add stock and stir to get bits up from the bottom of the pan to create a gravy. Return meatballs to the pan, cover and cook on low heat for 30 to 45 minutes or until gravy is thick. You may need to add a little water.

Serve with baked potatoes, Lee and Bo's Tomato Butter (page 186) and roasted carrots.

....

Kitchen Notes: These meatballs freeze well. Cool completely and place in a freezer container in a single layer.

Meat browns best in a cast-iron pan or Dutch oven.

To mix beef and pork, you can use a stand mixer with the dough hook attachment.

Aunt Nancy's Dry-Rub Ribs

Ribs are always a hit in our family. My aunt Nancy rightfully lays claim to THE superior ribs. Nancy swears by the "long low cook direct to grill" method, whereas my mom first braises her ribs at a low temperature in beer, then finishes them on the grill. After Nancy tested her rib recipe with our friend Bruce Good, they both declared that "these rock!" **SERVES 6 TO 8**

INGREDIENTS

3 strips baby back ribs (each about 2 1/2 lb/1.25 kg)

1/4 cup (60 mL) your favourite barbecue sauce (optional)

DRY RUB

1/2 cup (125 mL) brown sugar

1/4 cup (60 mL) celery seeds

4 tsp (20 mL) chili powder

2 tsp (10 mL) salt

1 tsp (5 mL) garlic powder

Pepper to taste

HOW TO

In a small bowl, mix together dry-rub ingredients. Press dry rub onto meat side of ribs. Cover and marinate, refrigerated, at least 3 hours or up to 24 hours. Bring meat to room temperature before grilling.

Preheat grill to medium-high.

Place ribs on grill meat side down, turn heat down to medium, close lid and grill for 10 minutes. Flip ribs, close lid, turn heat down to medium-low and cook another 35 minutes. You may need to turn the ribs a few times. Before taking ribs off grill, cut them into pieces of 2 or 3 ribs each. In the last few minutes, brush ribs with a bit of barbecue sauce, if using.

Serve on a warm platter with your favourite barbecue dipping sauce and with baked potatoes and Caesar salad—my pickiest younger brother Rob's perfect meal.

....

Kitchen Notes: Buy ribs as thin and lean as possible.

Ode-to-Ontario Pork Tenderloin

I have so many recipes for dressing up pork tenderloin, from Asian to Indian. But this recipe is one of my absolute favourites. It uses my dad's apples and maple syrup—an ode to Ontario!

SERVES 4

INGREDIENTS

1 cup (250 mL) beer

1/4 cup (60 mL) maple syrup

1/4 cup (60 mL) soy sauce

1/4 Vidalia onion, finely chopped

1 tart apple (such as McIntosh), peeled and finely chopped

2 tsp (10 mL) chopped fresh thyme

2 pork tenderloins (each about 3/4 lb/375 g)

Salt and pepper to taste

HOW TO

Preheat oven to 400°F (200°C).

In a small saucepan, combine beer, maple syrup, soy sauce, onion, apple and thyme. Bring to a boil, reduce heat and simmer for 15 minutes or until slightly thickened.

Season pork with salt and pepper and put in a shallow roasting pan. Tuck thin "tail" under so each tenderloin is a uniform thickness. Pour sauce over pork.

Roast uncovered, basting with sauce a few times, 40 minutes or until a meat thermometer reads 160°F (70°C). Let rest 5 minutes before carving. Slice into thick medallions and spoon sauce over top.

....

Kitchen Notes: Pork pairs beautifully with sweet flavours and with fruit. A great accompaniment is Baked Sweet Potato Fries (page 174). Also great with roasted peaches or pineapple or with applesauce.

Variations: For an Asian variation, make sauce from 4 sliced green onions, 4 minced cloves garlic, 3 tbsp (50 mL) minced fresh ginger and 1/3 cup (75 mL) each of soy sauce, honey and dry sherry. Serve with steamed rice and sautéed sugar snap peas.

A simple grill variation: marinate in ingredients above for 3 to 24 hours, then grill about 25 minutes (6 minutes per side).

Baked Ham

Ham was never my favourite as a child. I guess I have grown up! Last New Year's, we were hosting four families—eight adults and eleven kids. I needed something simple I could finish after a day of skiing. This is the perfect make-ahead, feed-a-crowd-in-two-seatings and look-very-impressive dish. And afterwards you get to enjoy days and days of ski sandwiches.

SERVES 10 TO 12

INGREDIENTS

1 fully cooked spiral-cut smoked ham (4 to 6 lb/2 to 2.7 kg)

3 cloves garlic, minced

1/3 cup (75 mL) brown sugar

1/3 cup (75 mL) mango chutney

1/4 cup (60 mL) Dijon mustard

2 tbsp (30 mL) fresh orange juice

20 whole cloves

HOW TO

Preheat oven to 325°F (160°C).

Place ham in a roasting pan. In a bowl, whisk together garlic, brown sugar, chutney, mustard and orange juice until combined and smooth. Spread glaze over ham. Press cloves in an even pattern all over ham.

Cover with foil. Bake for 1 hour or until ham is hot and glaze is browned, removing foil after first half hour.

Slice and serve on a platter with mashed sweet potatoes and green beans. Serve with Bo's Good Mustard Sauce (page 188) on the side.

Pork Chops on the Grill

Every April, David "Lub" and Beth Latimer invite our family and fellow recipe tester Kari's family up to Kilcoo Camp for a tradition of having the camp to ourselves before all the kids arrive. One year Beth made the yummiest pork chops on the grill—juicy and packed with flavour. She said she did nothing—just a bit of salt and pepper. The barbecuer took the credit—so thanks, Lub! Here's a sweet-with-heat surefire hit. You must go to the butcher and buy thick, good pork chops, with a nice edge of fat. Don't overcook them and you will be rewarded with the best pork chops ever.

SERVES 4

INGREDIENTS

4 pork chops, 1 inch (2.5 cm) thick

MARINADE

Juice of 1 lemon
2 cloves garlic, minced
1 cup (250 mL) honey
1/2 cup (125 mL) soy sauce
2 tbsp (30 mL) Worcestershire sauce
1 tbsp (15 mL) olive oil
1 tbsp (15 mL) chopped fresh thyme
1/4 tsp (1 mL) cayenne pepper or hot pepper flakes
Salt and black pepper to taste

HOW TO

In a small bowl, whisk together marinade ingredients. Rub over chops. Marinate chops, refrigerated, 1 to 3 hours. Bring to room temperature before grilling.

Preheat grill to medium-high.

Grill chops 5 minutes each side, then turn the grill down to medium and continue cooking another 10 minutes or until a meat thermometer reads 150°F (65°C). Let chops rest 5 minutes before serving.

....

Kitchen Notes: Pre-cut chops from the grocery store are usually thinner, so reduce grill time accordingly.

Variation: You can forget the marinade altogether and simply season with a bit of salt and pepper, a few squirts of lemon juice and a bit of crushed garlic before throwing the chops on the grill. Thick-cut veal chops are also delicious.

Shannon and Elena's Southern Pulled Pork

My friend Shannon loves to entertain casually and ends up drawing much of Cabbagetown with her Southern cooking, like her chili dip and this fab pulled pork—and lots of beer! Elena made superb pulled pork sandwiches at dish. They were a labour of love. Overnight in the fridge with a dry rub, then the day in the oven with a wet marinade. Elena and I added some of her flavourful secrets to Shannon's dish, and voila—easy, and packed with deep Southern flavour.

SERVES 8 TO 10

INGREDIENTS

1 pork shoulder or butt (2 1/2 to 3 lb/1.25 to 1.5 kg), trimmed of excess fat

MARINADE

1 cup (250 mL) ketchup

1 cup (250 mL) sweet apple cider

1/2 cup (125 mL) water

3 tbsp (50 mL) Worcestershire sauce

1/3 cup (75 mL) brown sugar

2 tbsp (30 mL) smoked paprika

2 tbsp (30 mL) chili powder

2 tbsp (30 mL) minced garlic

1 tbsp (15 mL) ground black pepper

1 tsp (5 mL) hot pepper flakes

HOW TO

Put pork in a slow cooker (or Dutch oven). In a large bowl, combine all marinade ingredients. Pour over pork, rubbing in. Cover and cook on medium for 8 hours. (If using a Dutch oven, cook at 275°F/140°C for 6 hours.)

When done, the meat will shred easily when scraped with a fork.

Serve with warm buns, coleslaw or green salad and your favourite fixings, such as chipotle ketchup (see page 133).

....

Kitchen Notes: After the pork is shredded, you may need to add more ingredients, depending on the taste. If it needs sweetening, add a couple of teaspoons of brown sugar. If it is too sweet, add more Worcestershire sauce and lemon juice. If you want a heavier barbecue flavour, add more chili powder. You will probably end up adding more ketchup too. If it needs to be thickened, take the lid off and continue to cook it, letting the water evaporate.

Variations: You could substitute hard cider or beer for the sweet cider.
For a simple burrito or taco, fill a tortilla with pulled pork and add refried beans, Jack cheese and salsa. Top with sour cream and cilantro.

Mustard-Crusted Rack of Lamb

My friend Christie's mother-in-law, Judy, gave her this recipe just before she and Kirk got married, so she could look after him. Lucky for him, in addition to running her own accounting firm, Christie is a fabulous cook. This is a perfect meal for special-occasion celebrations.

SERVES 4 OR 5

INGREDIENTS

1/3 cup (75 mL) fine dry bread crumbs

2 tbsp (30 mL) chopped fresh thyme

1 tsp (5 mL) ground cumin

1 clove garlic, minced

1 tbsp (15 mL) olive oil

2 1/4 lb (about 1 kg) trimmed frenched racks of lamb (2 racks, 7 or 8 ribs each)

Salt and pepper to taste

3 tbsp (50 mL) Dijon mustard

HOW TO

Preheat oven to 450°F (230°C).

In a small bowl, combine bread crumbs, thyme, cumin, garlic and olive oil. Season lamb racks with salt and pepper; spread mustard all over the fat side. Pat crumb mixture over mustard.

In a roasting pan, stand racks against each other so the bones cross each other and the crumb sides face out.

Roast for 20 to 25 minutes or until a meat thermometer reads 130°F (55°C) for medium-rare. Let rest 10 minutes.

Slice between the bones—each person should get 3 bones.

Serve with roasted asparagus (page 154) and buttermilk mashed potatoes (page 176).

Roast Leg of Lamb

This is a classic Easter dinner and a meal I often requested for a birthday or special-occasion dinner. I love the smell when it's cooking and always hope there are enough leftovers to enjoy the lamb curry on page 151.

SERVES 6 TO 8

INGREDIENTS

1 bone-in leg of lamb (6 lb/2.7 kg)

6 to 8 cloves garlic, peeled and smashed

1 tbsp (15 mL) coarsely chopped fresh rosemary

FOR THE GRAVY

1/4 cup (60 mL) all purpose flour

2 cups (500 mL) good-quality chicken or lamb stock

HOW TO

Preheat oven to 350°F (180°C).

Trim any excess fat from lamb. Place lamb in a large roasting pan. Using a paring knife, cut 6 to 8 small slits along the top of the leg and insert garlic cloves into each slit. Press rosemary onto the leg.

Roast for 2 hours (20 minutes per pound/500 g) or until a meat thermometer reads 140°F (60°C) for medium, 145 to 150°F (65°C) for medium-well.

Remove meat to a board and let rest 10 to 15 minutes while you make gravy (see page 117).

Serve with mint sauce and mashed potatoes—a must with the gravy.

....

Kitchen Notes: Unlike chops or racks, a leg of lamb is best served beyond medium-rare, as it sits better (unless it's very young) in the family of low, slow and tender roasts.

Curried Lamb Leftovers

I don't know which I love more, the special leg of lamb or this easy, flavourful curry made with the leftovers. Use leftover beef from a pot roast if you prefer. **SERVES 4**

INGREDIENTS

1 tbsp (15 mL) vegetable oil

1 cup (250 mL) finely chopped celery

1/2 cup (125 mL) sliced onions

1/2 cup (125 mL) diced button mushrooms (4 or 5 mushrooms)

1 clove garlic, minced

2 tsp (10 mL) curry powder

1 tsp (5 mL) Worcestershire sauce

2 cups (500 mL) cooked lamb, cut into pieces

1 1/2 cups (375 mL) lamb gravy (from recipe on page 150)

1/2 cup (125 mL) beef stock or water as necessary

Salt and pepper to taste

HOW TO

In a large sauté pan, heat oil over medium heat. Cook celery, onions and mushrooms until soft, stirring occasionally, about 5 minutes. Add garlic, curry powder and Worcestershire sauce; cook, stirring, 2 minutes. Stir in lamb. Turn heat down to low, add gravy and simmer 10 minutes. Add stock if needed and heat through. Season with salt and pepper.

Serve over steamed rice or egg noodles.

....

Kitchen Notes: The lamb gravy is key, so make sure you save enough gravy from the leg of lamb dinner. In a pinch you could augment with some beef stock and wine.

Curry varies greatly in heat. The fresher the curry, the less you need. I love Bolts brand—it's quite powerful, so I use only 1 1/2 tsp (7 mL).

Variation: My sister-in-law Nancy does a variation using ground lamb—a great staple to keep on hand in the freezer.

Sides

Simple 4 Wheel Farm Spring Asparagus

Grilled Corn

Grilled Lettuces

Dad's Sautéed Garden Greens

Wilted Spinach with Toasted Sesame Seeds

Mushrooms, Peas 'n' Tomatoes in a Pan

Mom's Stuffed Tomatoes

Roasted Cauliflower

Cauliflower and Bacon Gratin

Chuckie's Roasted Beets

Roasted Reds

"Candied" Parsnip Fries

Baked Sweet Potato Fries

Cottage Scalloped Potatoes

Roasted Garlic and Buttermilk Mashed Potatoes

Mary Leishman's Turnip Fluff

Parsnip and Potato Gratin

Ghislaine's Endive Stampot

Stewie's Yorkshire Puddings

Simple 4 Wheel Farm Spring Asparagus

Like late-summer local corn, local spring asparagus is fleeting, and so you want it every day, every which way, while it lasts. My kids love finding asparagus—it grows as an individual stem hidden in light grass or hay. Looking for it is a bit like an Easter egg hunt! **SERVES 6 TO 8**

Boiled

INGREDIENTS

2 lb (1 kg) asparagus, trimmed, ends peeled
1 tbsp (15 mL) butter
Salt and pepper to taste

HOW TO

Bring 4 cups (1 L) water to a boil in a wide pan; add salt.
Immerse asparagus in boiling water for 2 to 3 minutes. As soon as water just starts to turn colour, drain the asparagus. Top with butter, salt and pepper and serve.

Roasted

INGREDIENTS

2 lb (1 kg) asparagus, trimmed
2 tbsp (30 mL) olive oil
Salt and pepper to taste
1/2 cup (125 mL) grated Parmesan cheese

HOW TO

Preheat oven to 475°F (240°C). Line a baking sheet with parchment paper.
Put asparagus on prepared baking sheet and drizzle with olive oil; sprinkle with salt and pepper. Toss to coat.
Roast for 8 to 10 minutes or until softened. Sprinkle with Parmesan and serve immediately.

Grilled Corn

When corn is fresh-picked in season I could eat it every day, and a ton in one sitting. Corn on the grill is fun and deliciously flavoured with smoke—but of course it's equally delicious boiled.

SERVES 8

INGREDIENTS

1/4 cup (60 mL) butter, melted
1 tsp (5 mL) fresh lime juice
1/2 tsp (2 mL) cayenne pepper
Salt and black pepper to taste
8 ears corn, husked

HOW TO

Preheat grill to medium.

Combine butter, lime juice, cayenne and salt and pepper; brush evenly over corn. Grill corn, turning every 3 minutes, for about 10 minutes or until softened and lightly charred all over.

....

Kitchen Notes: When boiling corn, remember that fresh, just-picked corn will take only a few minutes, and 5 minutes is as long as you'll ever need to boil it. Serve immediately on a platter, covered with a linen towel to keep it warm, and pass the butter, salt and pepper around.

Grilled Lettuces

I once enjoyed grilled radicchio at Gio Rana's Really Really Nice Restaurant (aka The Nose) in Leslieville in Toronto and finally, after years, I tried it at home. Voila—easy, delicious, different.

SERVES 4

INGREDIENTS

4 heads endive
2 heads radicchio
3 tbsp (50 mL) olive oil
2 tbsp (30 mL) balsamic vinegar
1/2 tsp (2 mL) hot pepper flakes
Salt and black pepper to taste

HOW TO

Preheat grill to medium.

Cut endives in half. Cut radicchio in quarters. Carefully brush lettuces with oil.

Grill lettuces, turning once, for 6 to 8 minutes or until crispy and just turning brown. Remove to a platter. Drizzle with balsamic vinegar and sprinkle with hot pepper flakes and salt and black pepper; gently toss. Serve immediately.

Dad's Sautéed Garden Greens

One year Kate, the fabulous garden expert at my parents' farm in Creemore, Ontario, planted rainbow chard, and it was the most beautiful green I had ever seen growing. **SERVES 4**

INGREDIENTS

2 tbsp (30 mL) vegetable oil

1 tsp (5 mL) minced garlic

1/2 tsp (2 mL) hot pepper flakes

1 1/2 lb (750 g) collard greens, kale, spinach or Swiss chard, washed, trimmed and chopped

Salt and black pepper to taste

HOW TO

In a soup pot, heat oil over medium-low heat. Cook garlic and hot pepper flakes, stirring, 1 minute. Add greens, tossing to coat in oil. Turn heat to low, cover and cook, stirring occasionally, 10 minutes or until tender. Season and serve.

Wilted Spinach with Toasted Sesame Seeds

This is similar to Japanese spinach gomae or wakame (seaweed) salad. I always feel like Popeye when I eat this.

SERVES 3 OR 4

INGREDIENTS

3 tbsp (50 mL) sesame seeds

Salt and pepper to taste

5 large handfuls fresh baby spinach (8 oz/250 g), tough stem removed, rinsed well but not dried

4 tsp (20 mL) sesame oil

1 tbsp (15 mL) rice vinegar

1/4 tsp (1 mL) hot sauce

HOW TO

Place sesame seeds in a heavy frying pan; sprinkle lightly with salt. Stir over medium-low heat until seeds are light brown, about 4 minutes. Set aside.

Line a large colander with a kitchen towel. Rinse spinach well and put it in the colander to absorb some of the excess water.

Pack spinach, still a little damp, in a heavy pot. Cook over high heat, turning spinach with tongs, until just wilted but still bright green, 2 to 3 minutes.

Place in a medium bowl. Add sesame oil, rice vinegar and hot sauce. Toss to blend evenly. Season to taste with salt and pepper. Sprinkle with sesame seeds. Refrigerate for 1 to 3 hours.

Serve with barbecued short ribs (page 126).

Mushrooms, Peas 'n' Tomatoes in a Pan

I adapted this quick side from Sara Foster's *Fresh Every Day* cookbook. I love its earthy flavours and bright colours.

SERVES 6 TO 8

INGREDIENTS

2 tbsp (30 mL) butter

1 tbsp (15 mL) olive oil

1/2 red onion, thinly sliced

1 1/2 cups (375 mL) sliced cremini mushrooms

1 pint (500 mL) cherry tomatoes

3 cups (750 mL) fresh or frozen peas

Salt and pepper to taste

HOW TO

In a large saucepan, melt butter with oil over medium-high heat. Sauté onion until just softened, about 3 minutes. Add mushrooms and sauté, stirring frequently, until soft and golden, about 5 more minutes. Add cherry tomatoes and sauté a few more minutes. Add peas and cook, stirring, until tomatoes and peas are soft but peas are still bright green, about 5 minutes. Season with salt and pepper and serve immediately.

....

Variation: You can also toss all the ingredients on a baking sheet and roast at 400°F (200°C) for about 20 minutes.

Mom's Stuffed Tomatoes

These look special and are always a bit of a treat. They are filling enough to be a vegetarian main.

SERVES 8

INGREDIENTS

4 medium field tomatoes
Salt and pepper to taste
3/4 cup (175 mL) dry bread crumbs
3/4 cup (175 mL) grated Parmesan cheese
2 tbsp (30 mL) chopped parsley
2 tbsp (30 mL) chiffonade of fresh basil
2 cloves garlic, minced
1/4 cup (60 mL) butter, melted

HOW TO

Preheat oven to 350°F (180°C). Line a baking sheet with parchment paper.

Halve tomatoes crosswise and scoop out seeds and some of the flesh, creating a cavity to fill. Sprinkle with salt and pepper. Turn upside down to drain on paper towels for 5 minutes.

In a medium bowl, combine bread crumbs, Parmesan, parsley, basil and garlic. Drizzle in butter and stir to combine. Fill tomatoes to the top. Arrange on prepared baking sheet. Bake for 20 minutes or until stuffing is golden brown.

....

Kitchen Notes: To chiffonade, roll herb leaves tightly and slice thinly on an angle.

Variation: A great variation from my star tester Martha Mansfield is a stuffing of mayonnaise, Parmesan, chopped green onion and chives, broiled until golden.

Roasted Cauliflower

If you have ever had fried sage, you will know how good this dish smells in the oven. Sauté sage in butter, pour over cauliflower, then roast—so simple and comforting yet also quite elegant. Browned butter sage sauce is a classic combination with gnocchi. Here the dish is lighter, but no less divine.   **SERVES 4**

INGREDIENTS

3 tbsp (50 mL) butter

3 tbsp (50 mL) olive oil

1 tbsp (15 mL) chopped fresh sage

6 to 8 large whole sage leaves

1 head cauliflower, cut into small florets

Salt and pepper to taste

HOW TO

Preheat oven to 400°F (200°C). Line a baking sheet with parchment paper.

In a small pot, melt butter in oil over medium-high heat. Stir in chopped and whole sage and fry for a few seconds until a bit crispy. Pour over cauliflower and season with salt and pepper. Toss well.

Spread cauliflower on baking sheet and roast for 30 to 40 minutes or until golden brown.

Serve warm.

Cauliflower and Bacon Gratin

This is comfort in a dish and perfect alongside a green salad (to make up for the richness!).

SERVES 4 TO 6

INGREDIENTS

1/4 cup (60 mL) plus 1 tbsp (15 mL) butter

1 tbsp (15 mL) chopped fresh sage

1 cup (250 mL) chunky fresh bread crumbs

1/2 cup (125 mL) 35% cream

1/2 cup (125 mL) milk

1 tbsp (15 mL) all-purpose flour

8 oz (250 g) bacon, cooked until crispy, broken into small pieces

1 cup (250 mL) grated Gruyère

Salt and pepper to taste

1 head cauliflower, cut into florets

HOW TO

Preheat oven to 375°F (190°C). Butter an 8-inch (2 L) square baking dish.

In a large nonstick frying pan over medium heat, melt 1/4 cup (60 mL) of the butter. Add sage and bread crumbs and cook, stirring, until all the butter has been absorbed and the bread crumbs are toasted, about 2 minutes. Remove from heat.

In a medium bowl, whisk together cream, milk and flour. Stir in bacon and 1/2 cup (125 mL) of the Gruyère. Season with salt and pepper.

In a medium saucepan of boiling salted water, blanch cauliflower for 2 minutes. Drain and toss with cream mixture. Pour cauliflower mixture into prepared baking dish. Sprinkle with bread crumb mixture. Top with remaining 1/2 cup (125 mL) cheese. Dot with remaining 1 tbsp (15 mL) butter.

Bake for 30 minutes or until cheese has melted and top is golden brown.

Chuckie's Roasted Beets

My dad's beets are my favourite vegetable, hands down. They need nothing more than a bit of butter, salt and pepper—they do the rest.

SERVES 3 OR 4

INGREDIENTS

8 medium beets, washed and trimmed, leaving 1 inch (2.5) stem intact

1 cup (250 mL) water

1 tsp (5 mL) salt

Butter

Salt and pepper to taste

HOW TO

Preheat oven to 400°F (200°C).

Place beets in a baking dish just large enough to hold them. Add water and salt and cover tightly with foil.

Roast for 45 minutes or until a skewer goes easily through the beets. Uncover and drain off any water. Once beets are cool enough to handle, peel by rubbing skin with your fingers (wear gloves to prevent staining!) or using a paring knife.

Cut into wedges and top with butter, salt and pepper.

....

Kitchen Notes: Peeling beets is a bit of a mess. Peel them over the sink, wear rubber gloves, and peel the beets while they're still warm.

Don't rinse them before peeling, as some of the flavour will be lost.

Beets are versatile—you can roast, steam or boil them.

Try to find small beets and keep them whole. (I call for medium beets here only because small are harder to find.)

Enjoy in salads or on their own.

Roasted Reds

This recipe is inspired by a photo from Sara Foster's *Fresh Every Day*. This is an easy and pretty dish, colourful and unexpected.

SERVES 4 TO 6

INGREDIENTS

1 pint (500 mL) grape tomatoes

1 red onion, cut into eighths

1 lb (500 g) assorted small radishes (about 2 bunches), trimmed, leaving 1/2 inch (1 cm) stem intact

2 tbsp (30 mL) good-quality olive oil

4 sprigs fresh thyme

Salt and pepper to taste

HOW TO

Preheat oven to 400°F (200°C). Line a baking sheet with parchment paper.

Spread out tomatoes, red onion and radishes on baking sheet. Drizzle with oil. Add thyme, gently stir and season with salt and pepper.

Roast, without stirring, for 25 minutes or until radishes are soft but still colourful. Serve immediately.

....

Kitchen Notes: This is also delicious using radishes only.

"Candied" Parsnip Fries

When parsnips are roasted, they become so sweet and caramelized from their natural sugars that I always want to call them "candied."

SERVES 4 TO 6

INGREDIENTS

1 1/2 lb (750 g) parsnips, peeled, halved crosswise
 and sliced lengthwise about 1/2 inch (1 cm) thick
2 tbsp (30 mL) olive oil
1 tbsp (15 mL) butter, melted
1 tbsp (15 mL) chopped fresh rosemary
Salt and pepper to taste

HOW TO

Preheat oven to 400°F (200°C).

Place parsnips on a baking sheet. Drizzle with olive oil and melted butter; sprinkle with rosemary and salt and pepper. Toss to coat. Spread in a single layer.

Roast for 30 minutes or until golden, stirring occasionally. Keep an eye on them in the last 5 minutes—they can burn quickly. Season with additional salt and pepper if necessary and serve immediately.

....

Kitchen Notes: I love these with grilled lamb chops—a double hit of rosemary.
If your kids won't touch these, try mixing up your "fries"—half potato, half parsnip. Same goes with a root-vegetable mash—go half and half with potatoes, or even add celery root.

Variation: For even more sweet-candy effect, toss with 1 tbsp (15 mL) maple syrup 10 minutes before they're done.

Baked Sweet Potato Fries

These are great with grilled pork tenderloin or a steak. Kids love them, and they are good for you too. Kristi's kids Cassidy and Andie helped peel during testing. My kids Fin and Liv often pull up a stool, grab a peeler and pitch in—a great way to get the kids involved.

SERVES 6

INGREDIENTS

2 tbsp (30 mL) butter, melted
1 tbsp (15 mL) brown sugar
1/2 tsp (2 mL) nutmeg
1 tsp (5 mL) salt
1/2 tsp (2 mL) pepper
3 large sweet potatoes, peeled and cut into 1-inch (2.5 cm) thick sticks

HOW TO

Preheat oven to 400°F (200°C). Line a baking sheet with parchment paper.

In a bowl, combine butter, brown sugar, nutmeg, salt and pepper. Add sweet potatoes and toss to coat. Spread potatoes in a single layer on the baking sheet.

Bake for 40 to 45 minutes or until light brown and crispy. Watch them carefully near the end—they can burn quickly.

....

Kitchen Notes: You can cut sweet potatoes ahead of time: place sticks in a large bowl and cover with cold water; drain well and pat dry before using.

Variations: For a savoury alternative, replace the butter, sugar and nutmeg with oil and rosemary.

For another savoury variation, replace sweet potatoes with smaller Korean yams. Toss in a mixture of 1/2 cup (125 mL) honey, 1/4 cup (60 mL) soy sauce, 2 tbsp (30 mL) vegetable oil and 2 tsp (10 mL) chili powder. Bake as directed above.

Here's a simple baked sweet potato mash: Bake 4 pierced sweet potatoes in a 400°F (200°C) oven with a piece of foil underneath (to catch the drips) until soft, about 1 hour. Slip skins off. Mash in a bowl with 2 tbsp (30 mL) honey, 1/2 cup (125 mL) freshly grated Parmesan and salt and pepper to taste. Serve with extra Parmesan shaved on top. These are fantastic with Pork Chops on the Grill (page 146) or the Ode-to-Ontario Pork Tenderloin (page 143).

Cottage Scalloped Potatoes

Originally this recipe was Swiss Scalloped Potatoes from *The Cottage Cookbook*, my most well used cookbook. It's a compilation of recipes donated by the cottagers of Pointe au Baril on Georgian Bay, my favourite place on earth. Note there's no cream here—it's a nice lower-fat alternative to rich scalloped potatoes but just as flavourful as the classic dish. **SERVES 4 TO 6**

INGREDIENTS

4 or 5 large Yukon Gold potatoes

Salt and pepper to taste

3 tbsp (50 mL) butter

1 1/2 cups (375 mL) chicken stock

1/2 cup (125 mL) grated Gruyère

3/4 cup (175 mL) grated Emmental cheese

HOW TO

Preheat oven to 400°F (200°C). Grease a large casserole dish.

Peel and very thinly slice potatoes. It's best to use a mandoline for this (but protect your fingers!).

Layer some of the potatoes in the casserole. Sprinkle with salt and pepper and dot with some of the butter. Repeat for four to five layers. Pour stock evenly over potatoes.

In a small bowl, combine cheeses. Cover potatoes with cheese mixture.

Bake for 45 minutes or until golden and bubbling.

....

Kitchen Notes: Yummy with baked ham and mustard sauce.

Lots of make-ahead opportunities here—peel and slice potatoes and hold in water until ready to use; pat dry well. Or make ahead of time, bake halfway and cool (freeze if desired), then cook the rest of the way when needed!

Roasted Garlic and Buttermilk Mashed Potatoes

When I'm deciding what to order in a restaurant, the sides are often more important than the main protein. If I see mashed potatoes on the menu, that's what I'm having!   **SERVES 6 TO 8**

INGREDIENTS

1 head garlic

1 tbsp (15 mL) olive oil

Salt and pepper to taste

5 Yukon Gold potatoes, peeled and cut into 1-inch (2.5 cm) cubes

Bouquet garni (peppercorns, bay leaf, parsley stems and thyme sprigs tied in cheesecloth)

1/4 cup (60 mL) buttermilk

2 tbsp (30 mL) butter

HOW TO

Preheat oven to 400°F (200°C).

Cut top off head of garlic, just exposing tops of the cloves. Place on a piece of foil. Drizzle with olive oil and sprinkle with salt and pepper. Seal tightly. Roast garlic for 30 minutes or until soft.

Place potatoes and bouquet garni in a large pot of cold salted water. Bring to a boil, reduce heat and cook at a low boil until tender, about 20 minutes.

Discard bouquet garni. Drain potatoes and return to the pot. Mash with a potato masher just until mashed—don't overwork them.

Squeeze garlic from the papery skins and add to pot. Add buttermilk and butter; mash to desired consistency. Don't overwork. Season with salt and pepper.

....

Variations: This is just as yummy without the roasted garlic and without the bouquet garni. Revise according to how stocked your pantry is! Add a couple of chopped parsnips if you like.

To turn this into a simple gratin, mix with other winter veg such as turnips, top with cheese and bake until bubbly and golden.

Mary Leishman's Turnip Fluff

At Christmas my sister-in-law Nancy brings her mom's turnip fluff—who knew turnip was so yummy and popular! Add this to your Christmas dinner or any winter family dinner.

SERVES 8 TO 10

INGREDIENTS

3 medium turnips (7 cups/1.75 L mashed)

3 tbsp (50 mL) butter

2 eggs, lightly beaten

3 tbsp (50 mL) all-purpose flour

2 tbsp (30 mL) brown sugar

1 tsp (5 mL) baking powder

Pinch nutmeg

Salt and pepper to taste

1/2 cup (125 mL) chunky dry bread crumbs

3 tbsp (50 mL) butter

HOW TO

Preheat oven to 375°F (190°C). Grease a 9- x 13-inch (3 L) baking dish.

Cut ends off turnips. Using a sharp vegetable peeler or knife, peel turnips. Cut into 1-inch (2.5 cm) cubes.

Put turnips in a large pot of salted water and bring to a boil; reduce heat to medium and cook on a low boil until fork-tender, 20 to 30 minutes. Drain and return to pot. Using a potato masher, mash turnip. Stir in butter and eggs.

In a small bowl, combine flour, sugar, baking powder, nutmeg and salt and pepper. Stir into turnips. Transfer mixture to prepared baking dish. Spread bread crumbs on top and dot with butter.

Bake for 30 to 40 minutes or until golden and bubbling.

....

Kitchen Notes: Ensure your chef's knife is very sharp to make it easier to peel the turnip. Start by cutting off the two ends so the turnip stands upright and you have a flat surface to cut down from. Working your way from top to bottom around the turnip, cut away the outside. You can also use a vegetable peeler for this job.

If you're making this to accompany a turkey dinner, wait until the turkey comes out, then bake the turnip and serve immediately. If that doesn't work for you, bake for 25 minutes before the turkey goes in, then reheat for 15 minutes after the turkey is out.

At one recent Thanksgiving table our family had an argument about turnips versus rutabagas. I had to consult farmer Kate, who knows the most about vegetables. Turnips are white with a bit of a purple top; they are sweet and mild when small and young and are stronger in flavour when older and larger. Their cousin the rutabaga is yellow-orange in colour with a similarly earthy-sweet flavour; the smaller, heavier ones are best. Often grocery stores mix up the names, but not to worry—both are great for boiling and mashing.

Parsnip and Potato Gratin

My friend Ghislaine, a great home cook, loves to cook casual dishes that make you smile—this is one of many.

SERVES 4

INGREDIENTS

1 lb (500 g) parsnips (about 5 medium), peeled and cut into 2-inch (5 cm) pieces

1 lb (500 g) Yukon Gold potatoes (about 4 medium), peeled and cut into 2-inch (5 cm) pieces

1/4 cup (60 mL) milk

2 tbsp (30 mL) butter

Pinch cayenne pepper

Salt and black pepper to taste

1/2 to 2/3 cup (125 to 150 mL) grated Asiago cheese

HOW TO

Preheat oven to 450°F (230°C).

Put parsnips and potatoes in a large pot of salted cold water. Bring to a boil, reduce heat and simmer until tender, 15 to 20 minutes.

Drain and return to pot. Using a potato masher, mash parsnips and potatoes. Add milk and butter. Mash again, but do not overwork. Stir in cayenne and salt and pepper. Place in a small shallow casserole dish and top with cheese.

Bake for 10 minutes or until warm, then broil for a few minutes until cheese is bubbling and golden brown and gratin is hot. Watch it carefully!

....

Kitchen Notes: You can make this the day before. Once it's in the casserole dish, cool, then refrigerate. Before serving, bring to room temperature, then heat and broil as directed.

Variation: You can also do parsnips and potatoes as a simple mash.

Ghislaine's Endive Stampot

This typical Dutch hearty fall/winter dish is from my friend Ghislaine, who has a love and respect for good food. She manages to have her family together around the table for most meals. This is a simple and straightforward one-pot dish of mashed potatoes with seasonal and local vegetables. Ghislaine's favourite version is with endive. Make sure you use the curly green endive, not the white Belgian variety. Ghislaine showed up just as we were taking a photo of the all-white dish, and I suddenly realized she had meant green chicory—lost in translation!

SERVES 6 TO 8

INGREDIENTS

1 1/2 lb (750 g) Yukon Gold potatoes, peeled and quartered

1/4 lb (125 g) chunk bacon (3 inches/8 cm thick), diced

Salt and pepper to taste

1 1/2 lb (750 g) green curly endive (chicory), trimmed and diced

1/2 cup (125 mL) grated aged Gouda

HOW TO

Put potatoes in a medium pot of salted water; boil until tender, about 20 minutes.

Meanwhile, in a small frying pan, fry bacon until crisp. Drain on paper towels. Pour off all but about 1 tbsp (15 mL) fat from the pan.

When potatoes are tender, drain, return to the pot and mash until just broken up. Do not over-mash. Season with salt and pepper. Stir in endive. Stir in cheese, bacon and reserved warm bacon drippings. Taste and adjust seasoning.

Serve with grilled German sausages. *Smakelijk eten!* (Enjoy your dinner!)

....

Kitchen Notes: Endive is a big family with lots of varieties. The green curly endive—aka chicory—is what you need for this dish. It can be a bit hard to find, so you may need to hit the farmers' market or the greengrocer's.

Stewie's Yorkshire Puddings

I remember as a child, going over to our friends the Baldwins for family dinners. Stewie is a great cook, and we all appreciated her roast beef dinners. But it was the Yorkshire puddings I loved best. While they were still warm, we would rip them open and fill them with gravy—yum.

MAKES 8 TO 12 PUDDINGS

INGREDIENTS

1 cup (250 mL) all-purpose flour
1/4 tsp (1 mL) salt
1/2 cup (125 mL) milk
2 eggs
1/2 cup (125 mL) cold water
Vegetable oil

HOW TO

Sift flour and salt into a large bowl. Make a well in the centre and pour in milk. Beat quickly. Add eggs, one at a time, beating thoroughly after each addition. Beat in cold water until mixture is bubbly on top. Refrigerate batter for at least 1 hour.

Preheat oven to 400°F (200°C).

Put 1/2 tsp (2 mL) oil into 8 to 12 muffin cups and put in the oven for 5 minutes to heat the oil. Pour batter over hot oil in muffin cups, filling each cup three-quarters full.

Bake for 30 minutes or until puffed and golden. Do not open the oven or they will fall!

Serve hot right out of the oven with Sunday Roast Beef Dinner (page 130).

Accompaniments

Lee and Bo's Tomato Butter

Bo's Good Mustard Sauce

Mom's Red Pepper Jam

Quick Fridge-Pickled Cucumbers

Bonnie's Mustard Pickles

Bo's Cranberry Sauce

Dodie and Dawn's Strawberry Jam

Butterscotch Sauce

Lee and Bo's Tomato Butter

Every fall, Mom and Bo set up their tomato butter production kitchen. I don't make this; I just put my dibs in every year for a few jars. Take a Sunday afternoon to enjoy—and preserve—the preserving craft.

MAKES 6 TO 8 HALF-PINT (250 ML) JARS

INGREDIENTS

DAY 1
10 lb (4.5 kg) ripe field tomatoes

2 cups (500 mL) white wine vinegar

DAY 2
6 cups (1.5 L) sugar

2 cups (500 mL) white wine vinegar

1 tsp (5 mL) salt

Pinch cayenne pepper

Spice bag (3 cinnamon sticks, 5 whole cloves and 5 whole allspice tied in cheesecloth)

HOW TO

Cut a shallow X in the bottom of each tomato. Carefully place them in a pot of boiling water and remove immediately with a slotted spoon. Core tomatoes and peel them. Squeeze out excess juices.

Roughly chop tomatoes and put into your largest bowl. Pour vinegar over, cover and let sit at room temperature overnight. The next day, strain tomatoes in a fine colander, reserving 1 cup (250 mL) of the liquid. Discard remaining liquid.

Put tomatoes and reserved liquid into your largest pot. Add sugar, vinegar, salt and cayenne pepper; give it a good stir. Add spice bag. Simmer gently, stirring occasionally, for 2 to 3 hours, until thick and soft.

Prepare half-pint (250 mL) jars by washing at hottest temperature in dishwasher. Dry well and keep jars upside down on a clean tray until ready to use.

Fill jars with hot tomato butter to within 3/4 inch (2 cm) of the top. Place flat lid on top, add screw band and lightly tighten. Place jars in a large pan of boiling water, on a rack if possible to prevent jars from knocking against each other. Add water to cover jars by 1 inch (2.5 cm). Boil hard for 10 minutes. Remove carefully and set jars on counter to cool. Lids should "pop" and curve inward as they cool. If any jar fails to seal properly, keep in the fridge and use within a week.

....

Kitchen Notes: For any canning project, you'll need jars with new rubber-ringed flat tops and screw bands (such as Bernardin-brand jars and lids). Boiling the filled and sealed jars for 10 minutes in a boiling water canner (simply a large pot with a lid) will sterilize the contents of your jars and ensure they will last on your pantry shelf for a year.

Bo's Good Mustard Sauce

This is one of the older recipes I found in my grandmother Bo's recipe box. I love that "good" stayed in the name. This is a must-have with baked ham and scalloped potatoes.

MAKES 1 CUP (250 ML)

INGREDIENTS

1/2 cup (125 mL) sugar

1/2 cup (125 mL) cider vinegar

1 tsp (5 mL) dry mustard

3 egg yolks, well beaten

1 tsp (5 mL) butter

HOW TO

In a medium heavy pot, combine sugar, vinegar, mustard and egg yolks. Cook over medium heat, stirring, until thick. Remove from heat and add butter, stirring until combined.

Once cooled, this lasts in a tightly closed jar in the refrigerator for days.

Mom's Red Pepper Jam

This is absolutely delicious with cheese and crackers or with chicken. My husband, Bryce, finds a reason to use it on just about anything.

MAKES 6 HALF-PINT (250 ML) JARS

INGREDIENTS

12 large sweet red peppers, cored and seeded

2 small hot red peppers

3 cups (750 mL) sugar

2 cups (500 mL) white vinegar

1 tbsp (15 mL) salt

HOW TO

Mince sweet and hot red peppers by pulsing in a food processor. Put minced peppers in a large pot and cover with boiling water; let stand for 15 minutes. Drain well and return to pot.

Add sugar, vinegar and salt; bring to a boil. Boil until thick, 1 to 1 1/2 hours. Cool completely.

Prepare half-pint (250 mL) jars by washing at hottest temperature in dishwasher. Dry well and keep jars upside down on a clean tray until ready to use.

Using a preserving funnel, pour jam into jars. Place rubber-ringed flat tops and screw bands on jars. Boil in a boiling-water canner as for Lee and Bo's Tomato Butter (page 186). Cool, check seals and label.

....

Kitchen Notes: This makes a wonderful host or Christmas gift with your favourite cheese and crackers.

Quick Fridge-Pickled Cucumbers

These cucumbers are a staple at our family table, traditionally served at a Sunday dinner with a roast prime rib or pot roast.

SERVES 4 TO 6

INGREDIENTS
1 garden (not English) cucumber
2 tsp (10 mL) salt
1/4 cup (60 mL) white vinegar
1 to 2 tsp (5 to 10 mL) sugar
Freshly ground pepper

HOW TO
Peel cucumber and slice as thinly as possible (use a mandoline if you have one). Place slices in a small bowl and cover with salt, then cover with water. Put in the fridge for at least 1 hour.

Drain cucumber slices, rinse and drain again. Transfer to a serving bowl. Barely cover cucumber slices with vinegar, sugar and lots of freshly ground pepper. Serve at room temperature.

Bonnie's Mustard Pickles

My mom said, "You have to have a recipe of Bonnie's in the book." Her gang of friends all said, "You have to have the Mustard Pickles in the book." So I did what I was told!

MAKES 12 ONE-PINT (500 ML) JARS

INGREDIENTS

6 pickling cucumbers (each 3 to 4 inches/8 to 10 cm long), scrubbed clean
   and chopped (8 cups/2 L)
2 large heads cauliflower, cut into large florets
6 medium (or 4 large) yellow onions, chopped (8 cups/2 L)
1 sweet green pepper
1 sweet red pepper
3/4 cup (175 mL) pickling salt
8 cups (2 L) sugar
6 cups (1.5 L) white vinegar
1/2 cup (125 mL) mustard seeds
2/3 cup (150 mL) all-purpose flour
1/2 cup (125 mL) dry mustard
1 tbsp (15 mL) turmeric

HOW TO

In a food processor fitted with the slicing blade, finely slice cucumbers, cauliflower, onions and peppers. Transfer to an extra-large bowl. Sprinkle with pickling salt. Add enough boiling water to just cover vegetables. Cover and let stand overnight at room temperature.

The next day, drain and rinse well in batches. Put vegetables into an extra-large pot. Add sugar, vinegar and mustard seeds. Bring to a boil, stirring.

In a small bowl, combine flour, dry mustard and turmeric. Whisk in some of the hot vinegar mixture to make a smooth paste. Slowly whisk paste into vegetable mixture; stir well. Return to a boil, and boil, stirring, for 5 minutes. Remove from heat.

Using hot, sterilized pint (500 mL) jars, bottle mustard pickle. Place rubber-ringed flat tops and screw bands on jars. Boil in a boiling-water canner as for Lee and Bo's Tomato Butter (page 186). Cool, check seals and label.

....

Kitchen Notes: When boiling vinegar mixture, turn the fan on high—it's quite a strong smell! This is delicious as an accompaniment with ham or pork tenderloin. Bonnie's son Bryce loves to load this on his sandwiches.

Bo's Cranberry Sauce

I always thought this was Bo's secret recipe and that she had a few tricks up her sleeve. Then I realized she just uses the recipe on the bag of cranberries! Even my grandmother has some quick fixes.

MAKES 3 TO 4 CUPS (750 ML TO 1 L)

INGREDIENTS

1 cup (250 mL) sugar
1 cup (250 mL) water
2 cups (500 mL) fresh or frozen cranberries

HOW TO

In a medium saucepan, combine sugar and water. Over medium heat, bring to a boil, stirring until sugar dissolves. Add cranberries and return to a boil. Reduce heat and simmer gently, stirring occasionally, for about 10 minutes. Let cool completely.

Serve with roast chicken or turkey, in a chicken sandwich or with chicken pot pie.

....

Kitchen Notes: At Thanksgiving and Christmas you can find bags of fresh cranberries in the produce section. The rest of the year, you will find cranberries in the freezer section.

Double the recipe and put into half-pint (250 mL) jars to give as holiday gifts.

Offer to make the cranberry sauce for a family holiday potluck. It takes no time, it's so simple and it requires only a bag of cranberries, so it's low cost too.

Variations: You can dress this up by adding diced apple or pear and throwing in a cinnamon stick. Substitute brown sugar for the white and applesauce for the water.

Dodie and Dawn's Strawberry Jam

At my paternal grandparents Dodie and Pa's cottage on Lake Kashagawigamog, my great-grandmother Maud would remind my grandma Dodie and my aunt Dawn that "a cup of berries makes a cup of jam." This was in the days of picking wild strawberries along the back roads near the cottage. As a child, my berry picking MO was pick, then eat. Aunt Dawn was more diligent about picking; she also makes the best strawberry jam. I have been known to show up at her cottage boldly asking for a jar.

MAKES 8 HALF-PINT (250 ML) JARS

INGREDIENTS

6 cups (1.5 L) strawberries, washed and hulled
2 tbsp (30 mL) fresh lemon juice
4 1/2 cups (1.125 L) sugar
1 pkg (49 g) light pectin crystals

HOW TO

In a large deep pot, combine strawberries and lemon juice. Using a potato masher, crush the berries.

Combine 1/4 cup (60 mL) of the sugar with the pectin crystals. Stir into strawberries. Bring to a boil over high heat, stirring constantly. Add remaining sugar and bring back to a boil for 1 minute.

Remove from heat. Stir and skim for at least 10 minutes until the foam is gone. Cool completely.

Prepare half-pint (250 mL) jars by washing at hottest temperature in dishwasher. Dry well and keep jars upside down on a clean tray until ready to use.

Using a funnel, pour jam into hot, sterilized jars. Place rubber-ringed flat tops and screw bands on jars. Boil in a boiling-water canner as for Lee and Bo's Tomato Butter (page 186). Cool, check seals and label.

....

Kitchen Notes: Pectin occurs naturally in lots of fruits and vegetables. It's a natural product that is used to thicken jams and preserves. Gelatin-like pectin is added when the fruit doesn't contain enough of its own pectin to gel. If you don't want to use pectin, continue to cook until jam is reduced and thickened.

Butterscotch Sauce

A good butterscotch sauce trumps chocolate on vanilla ice cream. Seriously!

MAKES A LITTLE OVER 1 CUP (250 ML)

INGREDIENTS

1 cup (250 mL) brown sugar

1/2 cup (125 mL) corn syrup

1/2 cup (125 mL) 35% cream

1 tbsp (15 mL) butter

HOW TO

In a medium saucepan, bring all ingredients to a boil. Cook until mixture forms a soft ball when a
drop is dropped into a glass of cold water. Pour into a jar and cool.

Keeps in the fridge for a week.

Sweets

Berry Meringues

Mango Fool

Applesauce

Poppy's Cedar Point Raspberry Ice Cream

No-Ice-Cream-Maker Lemon Ice Cream

Spanish Cupcakes with Coconut Frosting

Bo's Lemon Pound Loaf

Summer Peach Crisp

Mom's Saucy Apple Cake

Georgian Bay Blueberry Boy Bait

Mom's Christmas Chocolate Roll

Cheater Pumpkin-Eater Pie

Bo's Milk Chocolate Pudding

Best Ever Cottage Chocolate Chip Cookies

Oatmeal Cookies

Peanut Butter Cookies

Stewie's Ginger Cookies

[more sweets]

Mrs. Wendy's Chocolate Macaroons

Mardi's Shortbread

Liz's Cabbagetown Biscotti

Auntie Mary's Brownies

Nanaimo Bars

Hello Dollys

Bo's Date Squares

"Forbidden" Desserts

Strawberry Angel Dessert

Sherry Cake

Ice Cream Torte

Bernie and Foofie's Chocolate Chews

Double Chocolate Peppermint Bark

Kathy's Sweet Marie Bars

Chocolate-Covered Peanut Butter Balls

Berry Meringues

These meringues are beautiful and seasonal and perfect for a party. My favourite topping is strawberries in June, but raspberries, blackberries, blueberries or a mix are delicious too.

SERVES 8

INGREDIENTS

4 egg whites, at room temperature

1/4 tsp (1 mL) cream of tartar

1/4 tsp (1 mL) salt

1 cup (250 mL) plus 2 tsp (10 mL) sugar

2 cups (500 mL) 35% cream

1 tsp (5 mL) vanilla

2 cups (500 mL) fresh berries

HOW TO

Preheat oven to 250°F (120°C). Line a baking sheet with parchment paper.

In a large bowl, beat egg whites until foamy. Add cream of tartar and salt and beat until soft peaks form. Beat in 1 cup (250 mL) of the sugar, a little at a time, until stiff, glossy peaks form.

Place 8 small mounds, or a single 10-inch (25 cm) circle, on the baking sheet. Using the back of a spoon, lightly swirl and flatten into circles.

Bake for 1 1/2 hours or until meringue is just set and dry; turn down the heat if any colour appears. Cool on rack.

In a medium bowl, whip cream to soft peaks. Just before it's done, add vanilla and remaining 2 tsp (10 mL) sugar; whip to stiff peaks. Spread whipped cream over meringues and top with berries.

....

Kitchen Notes: My grandmother Bo says never make meringues on a wet or humid day. You need a dry day for dry meringues. She also suggests that once the meringues are done, turn the oven off and leave them in the oven overnight to completely dry them out.

Variation: Make bite-size kisses and dip them in melted chocolate.

My sister-in law Amy Halpenny shared her family's favourite strawberry recipes. At their cottage on the Big Rideau Lake, her Nana Halpenny would make a classic strawberry shortcake. Their communal strawberry sharing includes a bowl of hulled strawberries, a bowl of sour cream and a bowl of brown sugar. Dip, dip and repeat until you run out! Amy's sister Kate macerates strawberries in white sugar in the fridge for an hour, adding a few tablespoons of good balsamic vinegar and a hefty pinch of black pepper before serving.

Mango Fool

Make this simple, no-cook dessert when it's too hot to turn on the oven.

SERVES 4

INGREDIENTS

2/3 cup (150 mL) 35% cream

3 tbsp (50 mL) honey

2 tsp (10 mL) vanilla

1 cup (250 mL) canned mango pulp

2 ripe mangoes, peeled and diced

1/2 cup (125 mL) diced fresh pineapple

1/2 bunch fresh mint, chopped, for garnish

HOW TO

Whip cream until soft peaks form. Add honey and vanilla and continue to whip until incorporated and holding peaks. Gently fold in mango pulp.

Toss together diced mango and pineapple.

In champagne flutes or parfait glasses, alternate layers of diced fruit and mango cream, making two or three layers of each and ending with cream.

Chill for 30 minutes before serving. Serve garnished with mint.

....

Kitchen Notes: 1 cup (250 mL) 35% cream yields 2 cups (500 mL) whipped cream.
I like the small, yellow Alphonso mangoes best. They are sweet and have more flavour.

Applesauce

You have so many choices with what type of apple you can use. I am lucky to have a variety from my dad's orchard. Come fall, we are looking for lots of ways to enjoy apples. I used to make this when my son, Fin, was a baby, and apples are still one of his favourites. So simple and yummy.

MAKES 2 CUPS (500 ML)

INGREDIENTS

4 small apples
1/4 cup (60 mL) water
Pinch cinnamon
1 tsp (5 mL) maple syrup or sugar (optional)

HOW TO

Peel apples, quarter them and cut out the core. Cut apples into chunks. You should have about 3 cups (750 mL).

In a medium saucepan, bring apples, water and cinnamon to a boil, then turn heat down to low, cover and simmer, stirring periodically, until soft, about 20 minutes.

Mash with a potato masher if you like a smoother texture.

Depending on the sweetness of your apples, you may need to add maple syrup or sugar.

Enjoy as is or over vanilla ice cream.

....

Kitchen Notes: This makes a great compote to accompany roasted or grilled pork tenderloin.
If peeling and cutting apples ahead of time, hold them in lemon juice and water to prevent browning.
Experiment with different apples—this is great with Golden Delicious or red Cortlands.

Poppy's Cedar Point Raspberry Ice Cream

While my father-in-law, Lionel, is good at many things (kite-boarding and loading the dishwasher), you don't typically see him as a contributor to meals—except when it comes to his raspberry ice cream. Judi picks up fresh raspberries from the roadside stand and leaves them on the counter with a sticky note reading "Ice cream, please." Lionel always uses 35% cream, but I've made a calorie-counting adjustment.   **MAKES 1 QUART (1 L)**

INGREDIENTS

2 eggs

2/3 cup (150 mL) sugar

2 cups (500 mL) 10% cream

1 cup (250 mL) milk

2 tbsp (30 mL) vanilla

2 cups (500 mL) raspberries

HOW TO

Beat eggs with sugar until creamy. Add cream, milk and vanilla; beat well. Stir in raspberries. Pour into ice cream maker and freeze according to manufacturer's instructions.

....

Kitchen Notes: This can be made 1 hour before eating or days in advance.

No-Ice-Cream-Maker Lemon Ice Cream

This is so simple, quick and refreshing—no ice cream maker required! I've made it so often, I forgot that the original recipe came from *The Cottage Cookbook*. **SERVES 6 TO 8**

INGREDIENTS

1 cup (250 mL) 10% cream
1 cup (250 mL) 35% cream
1 cup (250 mL) sugar
2 tbsp (30 mL) lemon zest
1/3 cup (75 mL) fresh lemon juice

HOW TO

In a large bowl, combine 10% cream and 35% cream. Beat with an electric mixer at medium-high speed until cream starts to thicken slightly, 4 to 5 minutes. Add sugar and beat until incorporated. Stir in lemon zest and juice.
Pour into an 8-inch (2 L) square cake pan. Cover and freeze until firm, about 24 hours.
Serve with fresh berries.

....

Kitchen Notes: For a fun garnish, make frozen candied lemon curls: Use a vegetable peeler to make lemon peel curls, shake in a small bowl of sugar and freeze in a single layer on a small baking sheet.

Variation: For a lower-fat version, omit 35% cream and use 2 cups (500 mL) 10% cream.

Spanish Cupcakes
with Coconut Frosting

If you have my first book, *dish entertains*, you may have tried the Spanish Cake. This is the same cake base turned into cupcakes, with a coconut topping. These are the perfect pretty and delicious birthday-party cupcake for kids. They look like tropical pompoms.

MAKES 12 TO 18 CUPCAKES

INGREDIENTS

1 cup (250 mL) all-purpose flour

1 tsp (5 mL) baking powder

1 tsp (5 mL) cinnamon

1/2 cup (125 mL) butter, at room temperature

1 cup (250 mL) sugar

2 large eggs, separated

1/2 cup (125 mL) milk

FROSTING

3 tbsp (50 mL) butter

1 cup (250 mL) brown sugar

3 tbsp (50 mL) 35% cream

3/4 cup (175 mL) shredded coconut

HOW TO

Preheat oven to 350°F (180°C). Line a muffin pan with paper liners.

Sift together flour, baking powder and cinnamon.

In a large bowl, beat butter with sugar until fluffy. In a separate bowl, lightly beat egg yolks. Beat yolks into butter mixture until combined well.

Add flour mixture to butter mixture alternately with milk, combining well after each addition.

In a separate bowl with clean beaters, beat egg whites until soft peaks form. Gently but thoroughly fold egg whites into batter. Spoon batter into liners, filling three-quarters full.

Bake for 20 minutes or until cupcakes spring back when touched and top is light golden.

Cool cupcakes in pan on rack for 5 minutes. Remove from pan and cool completely before icing.

To make the frosting, in a medium saucepan, melt butter. Add sugar and simmer, stirring, for 2 minutes. Stir in cream. Bring to a boil, stirring. Remove from heat and stir in 1/2 cup (125 mL) of the coconut. Cool.

Ice cooled cupcakes with frosting and sprinkle with remaining coconut.

....

Kitchen Notes: Make a maple-flavoured or "Spanish" frosting by using 1/4 cup (60 mL) butter, 1/2 cup (125 mL) brown sugar, 2 tbsp (30 mL) milk and 1 cup (250 mL) icing sugar. Follow the same method.

Bo's Lemon Pound Loaf

This is so moist, even the non-lemon lovers will be won over. You could even convince yourself this is a breakfast treat!

MAKES 1 LOAF

INGREDIENTS

1 1/2 cups (375 mL) sifted all-purpose flour

1 tsp (5 mL) baking powder

1/2 tsp (2 mL) salt

6 tbsp (90 mL) butter, at room temperature

1 1/3 cups (325 mL) sugar

1 tbsp (15 mL) lemon zest (1 lemon)

2 eggs

1/2 cup (125 mL) milk

GLAZE

Juice of 1 lemon

1/3 cup (75 mL) sugar

HOW TO

Preheat oven to 325°F (160°C). Butter and flour an 8- x 4-inch (1.5 L) loaf pan.

Sift together flour, baking powder and salt.

In a large bowl, beat butter, sugar and lemon zest until fluffy. Beat in eggs.

Alternately add flour mixture and milk, making 3 additions of flour and 2 of milk. Stir just to incorporate after each addition. Turn batter into loaf pan.

Bake for 1 1/4 hours, testing after 1 hour, or until cake springs back when lightly touched. Remove from oven and let sit for 10 minutes. Using a thin skewer or toothpick, poke holes in top of loaf.

To make the glaze, stir lemon juice and sugar together until sugar dissolves. Pour over loaf. Let stand for 20 minutes before turning out and cooling completely on a rack.

....

Variation: Dress this up with 2 tbsp (30 mL) poppy seeds added after the milk and flour.

Summer Peach Crisp

When local peaches are ripe, there really isn't anything sweeter and more flavourful. Combine peaches with blueberries and you've got a perfect summer fling. When I was at Camp Oconto, my favourite meal was the peach crisp we made ourselves on our cookouts. We'd pour a can of peaches into a frying pan, top them with brown sugar, butter and oats, and cook it over the fire. This is simply a fresh version. The kids love to make it—and of course eat it too!

SERVES 4 TO 6

INGREDIENTS

4 cups (1 L) sliced peeled peaches (10 to 12 peaches)
1 cup (250 mL) fresh or frozen blueberries (optional)
1 tbsp (15 mL) all-purpose flour
1/4 cup (60 mL) sugar

TOPPING

1 cup (250 mL) quick-cooking rolled oats
3/4 cup (175 mL) brown sugar
1/2 cup (125 mL) all-purpose flour
1/2 cup (125 mL) cold butter

HOW TO

Preheat oven to 375°F (190°C). Lightly grease an 8-inch (2 L) square cake pan.

Gently toss peaches and blueberries with flour. Taste fruit for sweetness before adding the sugar (3 tbsp/50 mL will be enough if you're eating this with ice cream). Spoon fruit mixture into prepared pan.

To make the topping, in a bowl combine oats, sugar and flour. Grate cold butter over the mixture. Rub in well with fingertips. Sprinkle over fruit.

Bake for 25 to 30 minutes or until golden brown and bubbling.

Serve warm with ice cream.

....

Kitchen Notes: Try peaches grilled with pork tenderloin and fresh peaches with vanilla ice cream. My grandmother always peels her peaches by carefully dropping them in boiling water, removing quickly and peeling while hot with a paring knife. The skin just slides off.

Mom's Saucy Apple Cake

This is yet another family dessert favourite. The kids love the sauce—but what's not to love about sugar and butter! When apple season hits, my dad's orchard yields way more than "an apple a day," so here is a sweet ending.

SERVES 8

INGREDIENTS

1 cup (250 mL) sugar

1/4 cup (60 mL) butter, cubed,
   at room temperature

2 eggs

1 cup (250 mL) all-purpose flour

1 tsp (5 mL) cinnamon

1 tsp (5 mL) baking soda

1/4 tsp (1 mL) salt

2 cups (500 mL) chopped peeled apples
   (McIntosh or Gala)

SAUCE

1/2 cup (125 mL) brown sugar

1/2 cup (125 mL) white sugar

1/2 cup (125 mL) 18% cream

1/4 cup (60 mL) butter

HOW TO

Preheat oven to 350°F (180°C). Grease a 9-inch (2.5 L) square cake pan.

In a large bowl, beat together sugar, butter and eggs until light and fluffy.

Combine flour, cinnamon, baking soda and salt. Stir into batter with apples. Spread in prepared pan.

Bake for 30 to 40 minutes or until centre of cake springs back when lightly touched or a toothpick comes out clean.

To make the sauce, combine sauce ingredients in a small saucepan. Bring to a gentle boil and cook, stirring, until slightly thickened.

Serve cake warm with warm sauce.

....

Kitchen Notes: Cooking in season is easy when you keep a list of ten ways to serve your favourite seasonal ingredients. For example, apples ten ways: apple pancakes, dried apples for granola, apples with pork tenderloin, apples in a spinach salad, apples in a smoked trout and mâche salad, fruit kabobs, fruit and chocolate fondue, applesauce, apple cake and, of course, an apple in my pocket for the perfect afternoon snack.

If by lucky chance you have any sauce left over, it's divine on top of vanilla ice cream.

Georgian Bay Blueberry Boy Bait

My mom spends hours picking wild blueberries on the Georgian Bay rocks for this cake—and then it disappears in moments!

SERVES 10

INGREDIENTS
2/3 cup (150 mL) butter, at room temperature
1 1/2 cups (375 mL) sugar
2 eggs
1 cup (250 mL) milk
2 cups (500 mL) all-purpose flour
2 tsp (10 mL) baking powder
1 tsp (5 mL) salt
1 cup (250 mL) fresh or drained thawed frozen blueberries

TOPPING
1/4 cup (60 mL) sugar
1/2 tsp (2 mL) cinnamon

HOW TO
Preheat oven to 350°F (180°C). Butter and flour a 9- x 13-inch (3 L) baking pan.

In a large bowl, beat butter and sugar until fluffy. Add eggs. Beat until light and fluffy. Beat in milk, flour, baking powder and salt. Spread batter evenly in prepared pan. Arrange blueberries on top.

To make the topping, combine sugar and cinnamon. Sprinkle over berries.

Bake for 40 minutes or until centre of cake springs back when pressed.

Serve warm with vanilla ice cream.

Mom's Christmas Chocolate Roll

This is my mom's version of a Yuletide log, a Christmas tradition at the Magwood table. It's far more casual than the usual fancy version, and so delicious. Now that our family numbers ten adults and ten kids, she may need to make three! The chocolate sauce comes from a cookbook of my great-grandmother's.

SERVES 6

INGREDIENTS

6 tbsp (90 mL) sifted cake-and-pastry flour

6 tbsp (90 mL) sifted cocoa powder

1/2 tsp (2 mL) baking powder

1/4 tsp (1 mL) salt

4 large eggs, separated

1 tsp (5 mL) vanilla

3/4 cup (175 mL) sugar, sifted

FILLING

1 cup (250 mL) 35% cream

2 tsp (10 mL) sugar

CHOCOLATE SAUCE

1 1/2 cups (375 mL) sugar

6 tbsp (90 mL) cocoa powder

4 tsp (20 mL) cornstarch

1 1/2 cups (375 mL) boiling water

2 tsp (10 mL) vanilla

HOW TO

Preheat oven to 400°F (200°C). Grease a 17- x 11-inch (43 x 28 cm) jelly roll pan and line with parchment paper or greased waxed paper.

Sift together flour, cocoa powder, baking powder and salt. Sift three more times.

Lightly beat egg yolks with vanilla.

In a large bowl with clean beaters, beat egg whites until they hold stiff peaks. Gently but thoroughly fold in sugar. Fold in egg yolks. Fold in dry ingredients until no flour is visible. Spread batter evenly in prepared pan.

Bake for 11 to 13 minutes or until cake springs back when lightly touched.

Turn cake out right away onto a damp tea towel and roll up with the tea towel. (This keeps the cake moist while it awaits filling.) Cover with a second damp tea towel and set aside to cool.

To make the filling, whip cream to soft peaks. Just before it's done, add sugar and continue whipping to incorporate.

Half an hour before serving, unroll cake. Cover with two-thirds of the whipped cream. Roll back up (without towel!). Put on a platter. Top with remaining whipped cream. Refrigerate.

Just before serving, make the chocolate sauce: In a small saucepan, stir together sugar, cocoa powder and cornstarch. Stir in boiling water and simmer, stirring occasionally, until thick, about 15 minutes. Add more boiling water if sauce gets too thick. Remove from heat and stir in vanilla.

Pour warm chocolate sauce over the chocolate roll. Cut roll into thick slices and serve with remaining chocolate sauce.

Kitchen Notes: The cake can be made the morning of. Whip cream up to 1 hour before. Assemble 30 minutes before serving.

It's important to sift the cake-and-pastry flour and the cocoa before you measure them, and then again together with the baking powder and salt.

This amount of chocolate sauce is generous and intended to yield leftovers. Enjoy over ice cream. It keeps in the fridge for days. The chocolate sauce can be made ahead.

Cheater Pumpkin-Eater Pie

If you're not a pastry person (I'm not!), go ahead: buy the frozen crust. This is my favourite pie, so I try to figure out ways to stretch Thanksgiving and Halloween to enjoy it a few more times.

SERVES 6 TO 8

INGREDIENTS

1 store-bought frozen deep-dish pie shell (e.g. Tenderflake)

2 eggs, separated

1 cup (250 mL) sugar

1 tsp (5 mL) ground ginger

1/2 tsp (2 mL) cinnamon

1/2 tsp (2 mL) salt

1 cup (250 mL) canned pumpkin purée

1 cup (250 mL) whole milk

1 tsp (5 mL) butter, melted

HOW TO

Preheat oven to 400°F (200°C). Thaw pie shell at room temperature for 10 to 15 minutes.

In a large bowl, beat egg yolks until light. Stir in sugar, ginger, cinnamon and salt. Stir in pumpkin, milk and butter.

In a separate bowl with clean beaters, beat egg whites until soft peaks form. Fold egg whites into pumpkin mixture until just incorporated. Don't over-mix.

Place pie shell on a baking sheet and spread filling in shell.

Bake until crust lightly browns, about 25 minutes. Turn oven down to 350°F (180°C) and bake another 25 to 30 minutes or until a knife inserted in the middle comes out clean.

Serve with a dollop of whipped cream or a scoop of vanilla ice cream and a splash of maple syrup.

....

Kitchen Notes: This pie is rich, so you can stretch it to feed 8 people—especially after a turkey dinner!

This recipe doubles really well. I buy a package of two pie shells, and since the recipe asks for less than half a 28-oz (796 mL) can of pumpkin, I double it, bake both pies and freeze one.

Even after doubling the recipe you may be left with a little bit of leftover pumpkin. Use it in a pumpkin soup or add it to the carrot soup on page 31.

Bo's Milk Chocolate Pudding

I have vivid memories of my grandma Bo's old double boiler. When I was a child, if the double boiler was on the stove it meant chocolate pudding for dessert, or at least some other fabulous chocolate concoction. If you use a heavy pot and you keep an eye on the chocolate and keep whisking, you don't need to use a double boiler.

SERVES 4 OR 5

INGREDIENTS

2 tbsp (30 mL) sugar

2 tbsp (30 mL) cornstarch

2 tbsp (30 mL) cocoa powder

1/4 tsp (1 mL) salt

2 cups (500 mL) milk

4 oz (125 g) good-quality milk chocolate, chopped

HOW TO

In a 2-quart (2 L) heavy saucepan, whisk together sugar, cornstarch, cocoa powder and salt. Slowly whisk in milk. Bring to a boil over medium heat, whisking constantly, then boil, whisking, for 2 minutes. The mixture will be thick. Remove from heat.

Stir in chocolate until melted and smooth.

Transfer to a bowl and cover tightly, placing plastic wrap directly onto surface of the pudding (to prevent a skin forming). Chill until cold, at least 2 hours.

....

Kitchen Notes: Make sure you use the best quality chocolate you can find. I love Camino, Valrhona, Callebaut and Scharffen Berger.

Variations: This is rich enough as is, but if you need more, you can use 1 1/2 cups (375 mL) milk and 1/2 cup (125 mL) 35% cream.

Create a bittersweet pudding, swapping out the milk chocolate.

My grandmother likes this with a spoonful of grape jelly.

Best Ever Cottage Chocolate Chip Cookies

For years, I have been asked for the recipe for my "best ever" chocolate chip cookies. Well, here it is. The secret is to slightly underbake them, which keeps them chewy and tasting a little bit like that raw cookie dough we all secretly love. My sister-in-law Amanda has stolen the torch for making the best batch—I suppose they are a bit of a craft. My mom has to hide these from my husband or they disappear in seconds.

MAKES 4 DOZEN

INGREDIENTS

1 cup (250 mL) butter, at room temperature

1 cup (250 mL) packed brown sugar

1 cup (250 mL) white sugar

2 large eggs

2 tsp (10 mL) vanilla

2 cups (500 mL) all-purpose flour

1 tsp (5 mL) baking soda

1 tsp (5 mL) salt

1 pkg (300 g) semisweet chocolate chips

HOW TO

Preheat oven to 350°F (180°C). Lightly grease a cookie sheet.

In a large bowl, using an electric mixer, cream butter and both sugars until light and fluffy. Add eggs one at a time, beating well after each addition. Beat in vanilla.

Combine flour, baking soda and salt. Add to batter and mix on low speed until just combined. Stir in chocolate chips.

Drop batter by tablespoons onto prepared cookie sheet, leaving a good inch (2.5 cm) between cookies. You'll get 12 cookies per sheet. Dip spoon into hot water if batter sticks. Lightly press cookies to flatten.

Bake for 7 to 8 minutes or until lightly golden but still soft.

Let rest on the cookie sheet for 2 minutes, then transfer to flattened brown paper bags to cool.

....

Kitchen Notes: Brown paper bags from the liquor store, opened up flat, work brilliantly for cooling cookies. They absorb extra grease and so keep the cookies soft and chewy.

Pastry chefs always use unsalted butter, so they can better control the level of salt in a recipe. Older recipes never differentiated. I grew up in a house with salted butter. Even after ten years at dish, with all the chefs and pros and the fridge stocked with unsalted butter, I still reach for salted.

Variation: For butterscotch cookies, reduce white sugar to 1/2 cup (125 mL) and reduce salt to 1/2 tsp (2 mL). Substitute butterscotch chips. Bake for 8 to 9 minutes or until lightly golden.

Oatmeal Cookies

We always had a batch of these jumbo cookies in a cookie jar at the café at dish, and without fail, it would be the first place chef Elena would take my son, Fin, no matter what time of day it was. No wonder he has a sweet tooth!

MAKES 1 DOZEN COOKIES

INGREDIENTS

3/4 cup (175 mL) unsalted butter, at room temperature

3/4 cup (175 mL) lightly packed brown sugar

1/2 cup (125 mL) white sugar

1 large egg

1/4 cup (60 mL) water

2 tsp (10 mL) vanilla

3 cups (750 mL) quick-cooking rolled oats

3/4 cup (175 mL) all-purpose flour

1 tsp (5 mL) cinnamon

3/4 tsp (4 mL) baking soda

1/4 tsp (1 mL) salt

1 cup (250 mL) raisins or chocolate chips (optional)

HOW TO

Preheat oven to 350°F (180°C). Line a baking sheet with nonstick liner.

In a large bowl with an electric mixer, cream butter and both sugars until well blended. Add egg, water and vanilla and beat until smooth.

In a separate bowl, stir together oats, flour, cinnamon, baking soda and salt. Add to butter mixture and mix until just combined. Stir in raisins or chocolate chips, if using.

Using large ice cream scoop, scoop batter onto prepared baking sheet, leaving at least 3 inches (8 cm) between cookies. Flatten slightly with the back of a spoon dipped in water.

Bake for 15 minutes or until golden brown. Cool on rack.

....

Variation: You can healthy these up by adding a few teaspoons of wheat germ or flax seed—no one will be the wiser.

Peanut Butter Cookies

This is the old-fashioned cookie, which we don't see much anymore with all the nut allergies. These are so yummy they will remind you of being a kid.   **MAKES 30 COOKIES**

INGREDIENTS

1/2 cup (125 mL) butter, at room temperature

1/2 cup (125 mL) smooth peanut butter

1/2 cup (125 mL) white sugar

1/2 cup (125 mL) brown sugar

1 egg

1/2 tsp (2 mL) salt

1/2 tsp (2 mL) vanilla

1 cup (250 mL) all-purpose flour

1/2 tsp (2 mL) baking soda

HOW TO

Preheat oven to 350°F (180°C). Lightly grease a cookie sheet or line with nonstick liner.

In a large bowl with an electric mixer, cream butter with peanut butter until light and fluffy. Add white and brown sugars and beat until combined. Beat in egg, salt and vanilla. Stir in flour and baking soda.

Drop batter by tablespoons onto prepared cookie sheet, leaving a good inch (2.5 cm) between cookies. Press down with a fork.

Bake for 10 to 12 minutes or until lightly coloured. Cool on rack.

Stewie's Ginger Cookies

Yes, Santa, these are the soft, chewy ginger cookies you love. Our former baker at dish, Adell Shneer, used to add crystallized ginger or put a big chunk of chocolate right in the middle. Enjoy these all year round—ginger, after all, is good for you. **MAKES 3 DOZEN COOKIES**

INGREDIENTS

3/4 cup (175 mL) butter, at room temperature

1 cup (250 mL) sugar, plus additional for rolling

1 egg

1/4 cup (60 mL) molasses

2 cups (500 mL) all-purpose flour

2 tsp (10 mL) baking soda

2 tsp (10 mL) ground ginger

1 tsp (5 mL) cinnamon

1/2 tsp (2 mL) salt

HOW TO

Preheat oven to 375°F (190°C).

In a large bowl with an electric mixer, cream butter with sugar until fluffy. Beat in egg. Beat in molasses until well combined.

In another bowl, combine flour, baking soda, ginger, cinnamon and salt. Stir into batter until just mixed.

Shape into 1-inch (2.5 cm) balls. Roll in white sugar to coat. Place on an ungreased cookie sheet 1 inch (2.5 cm) apart. Do not flatten.

Bake for 8 to 10 minutes or until cookies just start to crack.

Let sit on cookie sheets for several minutes, then transfer to flattened brown paper bags or racks to cool.

....

Variations: For special ginger cookies, stir in 1/2 cup (125 mL) chopped crystallized ginger before shaping into balls.

For the chocolate lovers, once cookies are formed on the cookie sheet, gently press a small chunk of good-quality milk chocolate into the top.

Mrs. Wendy's Chocolate Macaroons

Every Christmas my sister-in-law Amanda arrives at my mom and dad's farm with a ton of baking from her mom, Wendy. These are one of my favourites from among her many treats. They're super easy and no-bake!

MAKES 4 1/2 DOZEN MACAROONS

INGREDIENTS

2 cups (500 mL) sugar

6 tbsp (90 mL) cocoa powder

1/2 cup (125 mL) butter

1/2 cup (125 mL) milk

1/2 tsp (2 mL) vanilla

3 cups (750 mL) instant rolled oats

1 cup (250 mL) sweetened flaked coconut

HOW TO

In a medium saucepan, combine sugar, cocoa powder, butter and milk. Bring to a boil, stirring. Remove from heat and stir in vanilla. Stir in oats and coconut until well blended.

Onto a greased or parchment-lined baking sheet, spoon 1 tsp (5 mL) of mixture for each macaroon.

Refrigerate until serving.

Mardi's Shortbread

For as long as I can remember, my dad had a fabulous assistant, Mardi. She was the real boss. She also made the best cookies at Christmas. My grandmother had Mardi's shortbread recipe in her file, and my mom makes these every Christmas. She calls them "long shortbread," meaning they're long on butter, making them melt in your mouth. These can sit in a cookie tin (if you have the willpower to resist) for weeks. In fact, they seem to get better with age.

MAKES 5 DOZEN COOKIES

INGREDIENTS

2 cups (500 mL) all-purpose flour
1 cup (250 mL) icing sugar
1 cup (250 mL) cornstarch
2 cups (500 mL) butter
1 tsp (5 mL) vanilla
Coloured sugar for decoration

HOW TO

Sift together flour, icing sugar and cornstarch.

In a large bowl with an electric mixer, cream butter until fluffy. Beat in vanilla. Gradually add dry ingredients to butter, beating on low speed. Cover and refrigerate for 1 hour.

Preheat oven to 300°F (150°C). Line a baking sheet with parchment paper.

Form teaspoons of batter into balls and arrange on baking sheet. Flatten with a fork dipped in cold water.

Bake for 20 to 30 minutes or until firm but not coloured. Wait a few minutes to let cookies set before transferring to a rack to cool completely. Sprinkle cookies with coloured sugar.

Liz's Cabbagetown Biscotti

Liz is my great friend from our old neighbourhood, Cabbagetown. For every potluck, party in the park or weekend road hockey coffee break at Liz and Steve's, Liz would whip up biscotti. They were never the same, always depending on what she had on hand—just the way simple fare should be. One of my first staff at dish and one of the best bakers I know, Adell Shneer, taught me to love biscotti because she makes them so well—lots of her tips are in here too.

MAKES 3 DOZEN BISCOTTI

INGREDIENTS

3 eggs
1/2 cup (125 mL) white sugar
1/2 cup (125 mL) brown sugar
1/4 cup (60 mL) butter, melted
2 tsp (10 mL) vanilla
2 cups (500 mL) all-purpose flour
1 tsp (5 mL) baking soda
1/2 tsp (2 mL) baking powder
1/2 tsp (2 mL) salt
3/4 cup (175 mL) chopped dried cranberries (see Variations for other ideas)
3/4 cup (175 mL) crushed pistachios (see Variations for other ideas)

HOW TO

In a large bowl with an electric mixer, beat eggs, white sugar, brown sugar, butter and vanilla until fluffy.

In another bowl, combine flour, baking soda, baking powder and salt. Stir into egg mixture just until combined. Fold in cranberries and pistachios. Cover and refrigerate dough until firm, about 1 hour.

Preheat oven to 325°F (160°C). Line a baking sheet with parchment paper.

Divide dough in four. Place each piece of dough on a lightly floured surface and shape into a slightly flattened log 3 inches (8 cm) wide. Arrange logs on the baking sheet.

Bake for 30 to 40 minutes, until logs are slightly firm and the tops have colour. Transfer to rack; let cool 10 minutes.

Turn oven down to 300°F (150°C).

On a cutting board and using a bread knife, cut logs into slices 1 inch (2.5 cm) thick and return to the baking sheet. Bake for 10 minutes each side or until biscotti are crisp.

Store in an airtight container and serve with coffee for dunking.

Kitchen Notes: Storage is key—leave biscotti on the stovetop to cool and dry out overnight. Do not put them in a container until they are completely dry.

Variations: Add anything you have in the cupboard. After adding the flour mixture, fold in 1 1/2 cups (375 mL) total of any of the following: sliced almonds, pumpkin seeds, sunflower seeds, pistachios, raisins, currants, dried cranberries, dried cherries, chocolate chips, lemon and/or lime and/or orange zest.

To fancy them up, dip one end in melted dark chocolate or melted white chocolate and roll in pistachios or chopped dried cranberries.

Auntie Mary's Brownies

When I was a kid, our parents' good friends were called Auntie and Uncle, even though they were no relation at all. Auntie Mary was my mom's great friend Pat's mom. Those Winnipeg women sure can bake! In my first cookbook, *dish entertains*, I have the best fudgy brownie recipe. It's intense, for the serious chocolate lover. This recipe is more old-fashioned and not as intensely chocolatey; it's perfect for those who prefer cakey brownies.

MAKES ABOUT 16 BROWNIES

INGREDIENTS

2 oz (60 g) unsweetened chocolate, chopped

1/2 cup (125 mL) butter

3/4 cup (175 mL) all-purpose flour

1/2 tsp (2 mL) baking powder

1/2 tsp (2 mL) salt

2 eggs

1 cup (250 mL) sugar

2 tbsp (30 mL) corn syrup

1 tsp (5 mL) vanilla

HOW TO

Preheat oven to 350°F (180°C). Grease an 8-inch (2 L) square cake pan.

In a small pot over low heat, melt chocolate and butter, stirring until smooth. Let cool.

Sift together flour, baking powder and salt.

In a medium bowl, beat eggs with an electric mixer; gradually beat in sugar until mixture is thick and fluffy. Stir in chocolate mixture. Fold in dry ingredients. Stir in corn syrup and vanilla. Spread in prepared pan.

Bake for 25 minutes or until a toothpick inserted in the centre comes out clean. Cool in pan on rack. Sprinkle with icing sugar or spread with icing; cut into squares.

Nanaimo Bars

One year in university my friend Lynn Bushell and I spent a summer in Whistler, B.C., a beautiful spot surrounded by mountains and all things outdoors. But what I remember best are the Nanaimo bars Lynn and I made over and over again. **MAKES 20 TO 24 BARS**

BASE

2 cups (500 mL) graham wafer crumbs

1 cup (250 mL) sweetened shredded coconut

1/2 cup (125 mL) finely chopped walnuts

1/2 cup (125 mL) butter, melted

1/4 cup (60 mL) sugar

1/4 cup (60 mL) cocoa powder

1 egg

1 tsp (5 mL) vanilla

FILLING

1/3 cup (75 mL) butter

3 tbsp (50 mL) custard powder

1 tsp (5 mL) vanilla

1/3 cup (75 mL) milk

3 cups (750 mL) sifted icing sugar

ICING

5 oz (150 g) semisweet chocolate, chopped

2 tbsp (30 mL) butter

HOW TO

To make the base, combine all base ingredients in a food processor. Process until dough comes together. If it's not coming together enough, add 1 more tablespoon (15 mL) melted butter. Firmly press mixture into a 9- x 13-inch (3 L) baking pan. Chill while making the filling.

To make the filling, in a medium bowl with an electric mixer, cream together butter, custard powder and vanilla until smooth. Alternately add milk and icing sugar, making 2 additions of each, beating until very smooth after each addition. Spread evenly over base and chill well before icing.

To make the icing, in a small pot over low heat, melt chocolate with butter, stirring until smooth. Cool slightly, then spread over chilled filling. Chill until chocolate is set but not firm, then mark into bars with a knife; chill again until completely set (this way the chocolate won't crack when you cut it cold). Cut into squares.

Hello Dollys

This square is so easy to whip up when you have the ingredients on hand. It's hard to have just one!

MAKES 20 TO 24 BARS

INGREDIENTS

1 1/2 cups (375 mL) graham cracker crumbs

1/2 cup (125 mL) butter, melted

1 cup (250 mL) chopped pecans or walnuts

1 pkg (300 g) chocolate chips

1 cup (250 mL) sweetened shredded coconut

1 can (300 mL) sweetened condensed milk

HOW TO

Preheat oven to 350°F (180°C).

Stir together graham cracker crumbs and melted butter. Press firmly into an ungreased 9- x 13-inch (3 L) baking pan. Layer nuts, chocolate chips and coconut over base. Pour over condensed milk to cover.

Bake for 20 to 25 minutes or until light brown. Cool on rack, then refrigerate before cutting into squares.

Bo's Date Squares

I have been on the hunt for the best date square for some time. Gary, a fabulous cleaner at my brother's house, makes the best I have ever tasted. I was too shy to ask if I could publish his recipe, so my go-to recipe tester, Elena, and I started with Grandma Bo's recipe, which I adore, and almost doubled the amount of dates. Voila—these are pretty close to Gary's, if I do say so myself!

MAKES 16 SQUARES

INGREDIENTS

1 1/2 cups (375 mL) water

1/4 cup (60 mL) sugar

1 tsp (5 mL) fresh lemon juice

1 1/2 lb (750 g) good-quality dates, finely chopped

2 cups (500 mL) quick-cooking rolled oats

1 cup (250 mL) all-purpose flour

1/2 cup (125 mL) brown sugar

1/2 tsp (2 mL) salt

3/4 cup (175 mL) cold butter, cubed

HOW TO

Preheat oven to 350°F (180°C). Grease well a 9-inch (2.5 L) square cake pan.

Bring water, sugar and lemon juice to a boil. Reduce heat, add dates and simmer until they are very soft and jam-like, about 20 minutes. Remove from heat.

In a medium bowl, combine oats, flour, brown sugar and salt. Cut in butter until crumbly (do not over-mix).

Evenly press half the crumbs into prepared pan. Spread date filling over base. Top with remaining crumbs and press down.

Bake for 30 to 40 minutes or until light brown. Cool, then cut into squares.

....

Kitchen Notes: When buying dates, make sure they look moist and full, not shrivelled and dried up. You may have to taste-test to find your favourites. Good dates make all the difference.

"Forbidden" Desserts

The sweets that follow are completely delicious, but they do rely on more than their fair share of packaged convenience ingredients. Still, if you can set aside any prejudices you might have, you and yours will be in for some yummy treats!

Strawberry Angel Dessert

This dessert is *sooo* good, and the kids are for nuts for it. I just had to share it!

INGREDIENTS

1 angel food cake (store bought)

1 pkg (85 g) strawberry Jell-O

1 1/4 cups (300 mL) boiling water

1/2 lb (250 g) frozen strawberries, thawed (about half a bag)

2 cups (500 mL) 35% cream

1 tsp (5 mL) sugar, or to taste

1 pint (500 mL) fresh strawberries

HOW TO

Tear angel food cake into chunks and put into a 9-inch (3 L) tube pan or 10-inch (3 L) Bundt pan.

Mix Jell-O and boiling water in a large bowl until Jell-O is dissolved. Add thawed strawberries. Beat with an electric mixer until foamy and well blended.

In another large bowl, whip 1 1/3 cups (325 mL) of the cream to soft mounds. Add sugar and whip until stiff.

Fold strawberry mixture into whipped cream. Pour over cake pieces. Cover and refrigerate overnight.

Whip remaining 2/3 cup (150 mL) cream. Wash, hull and slice fresh strawberries.

Dip pan in hot water briefly, then turn out dessert onto a platter. Decorate with whipped cream and fresh strawberries.

....

Variation: My mother-in-law, Judi, does a fun variation. She macerates smashed fresh strawberries in a bit of sugar, then mixes in crushed-up meringue and whipped cream—a strawberry smush-up!

Sherry Cake

My mom used to make this cake all the time when I was a kid (yet another Winnipeg recipe). I still remember the smell of coffee and the delicious taste of this "cheater" cake. I remember being amazed at how quickly my mom could whip up this cake, and now I know why—a few little shortcuts. She was mortified that I wanted to put it in this book, but it's so delicious, boozy and pretty to boot. (I'm mortified that she and her friends used to eat boozy cake on weekday mornings!)

SERVES 12

INGREDIENTS

1 pkg (515 g) yellow cake mix

1 pkg (135 g) instant vanilla pudding

4 eggs

3/4 cup (175 mL) vegetable oil

3/4 cup (175 mL) dry sherry

1 tsp (5 mL) nutmeg

Icing sugar, for dusting

HOW TO

Preheat oven to 350°F (180°C). Grease a 9-inch (3 L) tube pan or a 10-inch (3 L) Bundt pan.

Put all ingredients (except icing sugar) into a large bowl. Beat with an electric mixer on medium speed for 5 minutes. Pour into prepared pan.

Bake for 40 minutes or until a toothpick inserted in the centre comes out clean. Cool on rack. Once cool, turn out onto a serving plate and dust with icing sugar.

....

Kitchen Notes: It's worth getting a tube or Bundt pan for this cake and the Strawberry Angel Dessert on page 241.

Ice Cream Torte

This is one of those desserts that make you say, "I remember this!" Many mothers had variations of this ice cream remake. It's an age-old favourite, and it makes a perfect birthday dessert.

SERVES 8

INGREDIENTS

8 oz (250 g) semisweet chocolate, chopped

1 cup (250 mL) 35% cream

1 tsp (5 mL) instant coffee granules

2 tbsp (30 mL) brandy

1 pkg (8 oz/250 g) chocolate wafer crumbs

3 tbsp (50 mL) butter, melted

1 quart (1 L) chocolate ice cream, softened

1 quart (1 L) vanilla ice cream, softened

4 oz (125 g) Skor chocolate bar, crushed

HOW TO

In a small heavy pot, combine chocolate, cream and coffee granules. Stir over low heat until chocolate is melted and mixture is smooth. Stir in brandy and set aside.

Stir together chocolate wafer crumbs and melted butter until well combined. Press half the crumb mixture into bottom and up sides of a 9-inch (2.5 L) springform pan. Spread chocolate ice cream over bottom. Drizzle with half the chocolate sauce. Sprinkle evenly with remaining crumb mixture. Spread vanilla ice cream over crumbs. Drizzle with remaining chocolate sauce. Top with crushed Skor bar. Cover and freeze until ready to serve.

Bernie and Foofie's Chocolate Chews

I used to make a variation of these no-bake treats in high school with my friends as the ultimate after-school snack. Now I make them with our kids at Christmastime—they love the simple assembly, and they are great teacher or host gift from the kids in the kitchen. Put in a little pastry box or Chinese takeout box and tie on a recycled gift card with brown wool string.

MAKES 3 DOZEN CHEWS

INGREDIENTS

1 pkg (300 g) butterscotch chips (about 2 cups/500 mL)

1 pkg (300 g) semisweet chocolate chips (about 2 cups/500 mL)

2 cups (500 mL) dry-roasted salted whole almonds

1 1/2 cups (375 mL) salted pretzels broken in half

1 cup (250 mL) raisins

1 cup (250 mL) dried cranberries

HOW TO

In a large bowl over a saucepan of gently simmering water, melt butterscotch and chocolate chips, stirring until smooth, about 10 minutes. Turn off heat. Add almonds, pretzels, raisins, and cranberries. Gently stir, making sure no water gets into the bowl. Drop teaspoonfuls onto a baking sheet lined with wax paper. Refrigerate until set, about 30 minutes.

....

Variation: The original recipe was with peanuts instead of almonds and fried chow mein noodles instead of pretzels—a great variation.

Double Chocolate Peppermint Bark

Packed in bowls wrapped in organza or coloured cellophane decorated with ribbon and candy canes, or wrapped in parchment with ribbon, this yummy bark makes a great holiday food gift.

MAKES ABOUT A POUND (500 G)

INGREDIENTS

8 oz (250 g) white chocolate, finely chopped

1/2 to 3/4 cup (125 to 175 mL) coarsely crushed candy canes (6 to 8)

6 oz (175 g) bittersweet chocolate, chopped

3 tbsp (50 mL) 35% cream

HOW TO

Line a cookie sheet with foil.

In a metal bowl set over a saucepan of barely simmering water (do not allow bottom of bowl to touch water), stir white chocolate until melted and smooth (chocolate will feel warm to the touch). Pour white chocolate onto prepared cookie sheet and, working quickly, use an offset spatula to spread chocolate to cover pan. Sprinkle with half of the crushed candy canes. Chill until set, about 15 minutes.

In a clean metal bowl set over a saucepan of barely simmering water, stir bittersweet chocolate with cream until chocolate is just melted and smooth. Cool to lukewarm, about 5 minutes. Pour bittersweet chocolate mixture over white chocolate. Using a clean offset spatula, spread chocolate in an even layer. Cover with remaining candy canes. Refrigerate until very cold and firm, about 25 minutes.

Lift foil with bark onto work surface and break into large chunks. Keep, refrigerated in an airtight container, for up to 2 weeks. Let stand 15 minutes at room temperature before serving.

Kathy's Sweet Marie Bars

These are a cottage staple, and they go quickly. I'm not sure who eats more—the grandchildren or the parents!

MAKES ABOUT 24 BARS

INGREDIENTS

1 cup (250 mL) brown sugar
1 cup (250 mL) chocolate chips
1 cup (250 mL) peanut butter
1 cup (250 mL) corn syrup
2 tbsp (30 mL) butter
4 1/2 cups (about 1 L) Rice Krispies

HOW TO

In a large pot, combine sugar, chocolate chips, peanut butter, corn syrup and butter. Stir constantly over low heat until chocolate is melted and mixture is smooth. Remove from heat and stir in Rice Krispies. Press firmly into a 9- x 13-inch (3 L) pan and chill for at least 1 hour before cutting into squares. Keep refrigerated.

....

Kitchen Notes: Judi heats all the ingredients in a big bowl in the microwave and doesn't bother with the stove.

Chocolate-Covered Peanut Butter Balls

My friend Rebecca's mom made these for her when she was a kid, and continued to make them for our university house of grateful girls. A few decades later Rebecca's son Henry eats peanut butter every day—that's how powerful these little morsels are!

MAKES 5 1/2 DOZEN BITE-SIZE BALLS

INGREDIENTS

4 cups (1 L) icing sugar
1 cup (250 mL) chunky peanut butter
8 oz (250 g) soft butter
1 tsp (5 mL) vanilla
1 pkg (300 g) chocolate chips (about 2 cups/250 mL)

HOW TO

In a large bowl, mix icing sugar, peanut butter, butter and vanilla to form a ball. Refrigerate in the bowl for about 1 to 2 hours.

Using a teaspoon or a melon baller, scoop bite-size pieces and roll in your hands to form balls. Place on a cookie sheet. Place in freezer until frozen solid.

In a small pan over low heat melt chocolate chips. Dip each ball in chocolate and set on waxed paper till set.

Index

Strawberry Dessert
1 angel cake
1 pkg. Strawberry jello
1¼ C. boiling water
1 pkg. frozen Strawberries (thawed)
½ pt. Whipping cream (thawed)
Break cake into chunks (+sugar)
Evenly cake into chunks - distribute
Mix Jello + hot water in bowl
Whip ⅔ Cream - add sugar - Fold in

Cookies

OATMEAL
1 cup butter
½ cup brown sugar
1 Csp. vanilla
1 c.

RED PEPPER JAM. Jean Funnell.
12 large sweet red peppers
2 small hot red peppers
1 T. salt
3 c. white sugar
2 c. vinegar
Put peppers "
boil slowly until through fine food chopper,
clear and thick.
Pour water over
Let stand over
night - let stand
night - let + drain

Delicious with cheese and crackers.

Poached Restigouche Sa
1 onion,
¼ cup ch
2 table
1 bay l
1 table
4-5 pound piece salmon, centre cut
2 quarts water
1 cup dry white wine
1 carrot, chopped
3 cloves
6 peppercorns
In large, deep
bay leaf, cloves, pep
minutes.
Fold cheese
salmon in the cen
cheesecloth. Lay
liquid. Fold the
Allow to poac
test wit
With

MULLIGATAWNY SOU

Apple Cake